The Jesus Code

Unlocking the secret meaning of his teachings

Ren Lexander

renlexander.com

The Jesus Code is part of **The Meaning of Life** series

Stay up to date with releases:

renlexander.com

Cover photograph by Brigitte Werner

DEDICATION

Dedicated to Doris A. Sargeant who wrote one of the very first local histories ever in Australia, *The Toongabbie Story*.

And was my mother.

Table of Contents of The Jesus Code

Resurrection

The most famous and impactful man in human history is also its most misunderstood.

This book is a quest to right that wrong. It is a quest for resurrection: to bring the real man and his actual teachings back from the dead.

But resurrection cannot happen without death. Readers will be called on to die to their existing theories and prejudices, their current cynicism or faith.

Out of this death and resurrection, you will come face to face with the real historical Jesus. This man has much more to offer your life than you have ever previously conceived. He was a great teacher but he did not teach faith. He taught the inner path of the transformation of the soul. He was a "mystic" and, in the course of this book, that annoyingly vague term will be resurrected into clarity.

Jesus is going to reach across two millennia to teach you the one true spiritual path: the path of the inner evolution of the soul. For some readers, this will spur the same emotions it spurred in his disciples and followers: relief, hope and inspiration. For other readers, it will spur the same emotions that it spurred in the Pharisees and chief priests of his day: resistance, resentment, confusion, anger, fury.

Death and rebirth do not necessarily come easily.

Something to upset (almost) everyone

"Do not think that I have come to bring peace to the earth."

- Jesus, Matthew 10:34

We are going to see that Jesus did not call his followers to faith but to the inner path of the transformation of the soul. This has profound implications for every Christian because it means that, to be true to the teachings of Jesus, Christians have to go beyond faith. Possibly this book will provoke widespread Christian anger directed at the author but step back and consider this: all I have done is to make plain what Jesus taught. If this book makes you angry, it is because you are angry at the historical Jesus and what he taught. Jesus himself admitted that he taught in code:

> And he said to them, "To you has been given the secret of the kingdom of God, but for those outside everything is in parables, so that they may indeed see but not perceive, and may indeed hear but not understand..."
>
> - Mark 4:11-12

To truly understand the teachings of Jesus, we have to crack the Jesus code. We have to decode unique expressions used by Jesus: "the kingdom of God", "the Holy Spirit" and "Son of Man". Only then can we become insiders – disciples who understand Jesus – instead of outsiders enshrouded by deliberately veiled parables.

This book also demonstrates the universality of the path that Jesus preached and taught: spiritual seekers separated by time, language and culture, have nevertheless experienced the same spiritual path, the same spiritual transformation. This universality presents a very deep challenge for most versions of atheism. How do those atheists who hold that there is no such thing as the spiritual explain this independent universality of spiritual experiences across time, place and culture?

My quest for resurrection

> If you're going to make connections which are innovative... you have to not have the same bag of experiences as everyone else does, or else you're going to make the same connections...
>
> - Steve Jobs

At the age of 26, I went through a depression. The worst of my life... to then. A business I started with a friend collapsed. It gutted me financially, emotionally, personally, socially. And it caused me to ask hard questions: *Does my life have meaning? Does any life have meaning? Why not just end it all? Would it really matter?*

I already had a Ph.D. in philosophy, so I turned to philosophy for answers.... answers that, over the years, proved worse than useless. And I started to jot down some early, crude notes for an article on the meaning of life.

Three years later, my life had turned around. I was traveling the country, having been commissioned to research and write the national manual on local government and the arts. I had a TV series under option. I was building my first home.

But there was one piercing thought looping around and around in my head. A thought that would not let go of me:

There has to be more to life than this...

There has to be more to LIFE than this...

There HAS to be MORE to LIFE than THIS.

This relentless, unfading echo pushed me into inner work, into "experiential psychology" … breathwork, dreamwork, Voice Dialogue…

I spent much of 1991 in a center where we were trained in how to guide such techniques and were guided on the path of our own inner transformations. There, in deep sessions of inner work, I experienced unbidden visions, feelings of ineffable peace and a singular and unexpected transformative experience, unlike anything I had ever experienced before or have experienced since.

After my journey in the center came to an end, I began to absorb the writings of mystics so as to make better sense of my inner journey: Meister Eckhart, *The Upanishads*, Plotinus, Carl Jung.

And it occurred to me that if Meister Eckhart was a "mystic" and a Christian, then possibly Jesus was a mystic also. So I turned to the Gospels and I saw that what Jesus said about "the kingdom of God" dove-tailed in with the thoughts of other mystics.

But it didn't occur to me to write a book on Jesus. I was committed to my ongoing quest to solve the meaning of life. At one stage, I thought I'd completed that quest in the form of a book called *Towards Meaningful Lives*. But I ripped that book apart and, over the decades, it transformed into a trilogy on the meaning of life spanning philosophy, psychology and spirituality:

- *The Eternal Question: What is the meaning of life?*
- *There has to be more to life than this. The psychology of meaninglessness*
- *The Journey of the Souls and the meaning of life*

In 2013, I believed I had finished this trilogy.[1] So I sent a proposal off to my preferred literary agent. I figured it would take about a

---

[1] Revelations I had in the course of writing The Jesus Code caused me to do a major rewrite and divide it into four volumes.

month for her to get back to me. So I had a spare month. I thought this would be an opportunity to thrash out a first draft of a book I had vaguely intended to do: a book on how Jesus was a mystic teaching the path of inner transformation.

When I started on the quest of writing this book, I was sure that I would find other soberly-argued academically-constrained books on Jesus having been a mystic.

There would be other books on this out there.

For sure.

Definitely.

At least one.

Absolutely definitely.

One at least.

I could not find one.

Not one.

I was shocked.

I am still stunned.

How could there not be at least one academically-serious book arguing that Jesus was a mystic?

Because of this unfathomable lack, I have been forced to conclude that this book is startlingly original. *The Jesus Code* is the first book to:

- Make a coherent case that Jesus never preached faith but, instead, was a mystic teaching the path of inner spiritual evolution;
- Properly decode the unique expressions "the kingdom of God", "the Holy Spirit", "baptism by the Holy Spirit" and "Son of Man";
- Make sense of every one of Jesus's parables;

- Make sense of the Beatitudes and reveal them as being a step-by-step guide to the path of inner transformation;
- Reveal the true meaning of the Lord's Prayer;
- And more.

If this shocks you with its claim to over-the-top originality... well... it shocks me too. It took a prodigious amount of inner and outer seeking to get to these understandings.

> "...seek, and you will find; knock, and it will be opened to you."
>
> - Matthew 7:7

Are you prepared to seek?

Are you prepared to die to the idea that you already know it all?

Are you prepared to join in the resurrection of Jesus and his actual teachings?

"I must preach the good news of the kingdom of God... for I was sent for this purpose."

Part I

In the beginning

The voice of one crying in the wilderness...
- Mark 1:3

The Wilderness

The wilderness lies outside civilization, beyond the normal constraints of normal society and the normal ambitions of normal folk.

The wilderness is where unreasonable people go: people with troubled hopes and unreasonable thoughts.

Still in the normal world, yet to cross over into the wilderness, Yeshua was approaching his 30th birthday. This is a time when people look at their lives and think about what might have been and where the rest of their lives might be heading. Sometimes they are content with their path but often discontent nudges at the edges of their spirit.

Yeshua had been born into a poor family. They did not have enough money to start a business so Yeshua eked out an average living going from building site to building site. His fellow construction workers did not see much that was remarkable about Yeshua. Maybe he was a bit more introspective than most of the guys, but he was basically a good worker: friendly, honest, liked a cup of wine, and seemed sincere in his respect for the Jewish Law. What they did not know was that Yeshua was inwardly troubled by a persistent inner voice... *There has to be more to life than this.*

When Yeshua first heard about the preacher preaching out in the wilderness, he had not paid much attention. There were teachers and preachers coming and going all the time. But, as he heard more, Yeshua started to suspect that there could be something different about this one. Unlike the prophets of old, he was not calling for the nation to change. Instead, he was preaching that each individual had to change – change on the inside. *What could that mean?* The preacher was claiming that there was more to spirituality than keeping to the Jewish Law, its rites and rituals and rules – the rules that kept everyone normal.

Discontented by his inner discontent, Yeshua set his face towards the wilderness.

When his current construction job ended, he turned his back on the streets and structures of the normal world and walked out into the wilderness – making his way to that one place out there that would sustain life – the living waters of the River Jordan.

There was already a crowd by the Jordan waiting for the preacher to speak.

The reports had not properly prepared Yeshua for what he saw. The preacher was the wilderness made flesh. His clothing was camel's hair barely held together by a leather strap around his waist. His beard and hair were wild. People said that he lived off locusts and wild honey. Yeshua was accustomed to seeing priests who wore the finest of clothes and ate the most expensive of foods from the best of plates. But the wilding appearance didn't put Yeshua off. Instead, it resonated. *He doesn't care what people think about him. He doesn't care about fitting in with expectations. He doesn't even care if people see him as a preacher.*

The preacher stood and addressed the crowd: "Wake up!! The kingdom of God is at hand!"

The slap of silence in the wilderness.

And the preacher spoke again. He told the crowd that he could baptize each one of them in water to symbolize their commitment to changing their ways but there was a much greater baptism: they could be baptized by the Holy Spirit.

Yeshua had never heard such expressions before. "The Holy Spirit"? "The kingdom of God"? "Baptized by the Holy Spirit"!? What the hell did those words mean? How could you be "baptized by the Holy Spirit"? What was "the Holy Spirit"? Normal people did not use expressions like that. Jewish scripture did not contain words like that.

Yeshua did not fully understand what this man meant but there was one thing of which he was certain: these were not just empty words to this preacher. This man talked with authority. He was talking from experience.

Maybe this man really did know the path to real meaning in life.

Yeshua looked at the preacher's disciples. Their edges had been roughened by the wilderness but their eyes sparkled.

The preacher tells the gathering of normal people that now God wants more from them than he demanded from their ancestors. God wants to harvest great souls – souls that have borne fruit.

Someone from the crowd asks the preacher what averaged folk could do.

(For not everyone is ready to embrace the wilderness.)

The preacher tells them to make a start by developing inner compassion towards all fellow Israelites. If they have two coats, give one away to the man who does not have a coat. Share food with those who need food. If they are in positions of power, they should only take their wage and not steal or extort more than is their entitlement. The preacher urges the crowd to be baptized in the River Jordan as a symbol for washing away their old ways and old sins and making a commitment to a new way – but only if they are truly committed to change.

Yeshua joins the queue to be baptized. *How committed to change am I really?* His mind was turning over the words of the preacher and not just his words but the surety behind those words. *There has to be more to life than cut wood, hammer nail. Can I really let it go? Embrace the wilderness? Become his disciple? For as long as it takes? But what about the comforts of normality? The normal food? The normal friends? My family might think I've gone crazy and joined a cult.*

It was so tempting for Yeshua to turn his back on the wilderness and head back towards the structures that contained familiar thoughts and averaged normality. But...

But there has to be more to life than that...

Now Yeshua was at the front of the queue. It was his turn to be baptized by water. The preacher very consciously and deliberately placed his hands on Yeshua's shoulders to guide his body through the immersion. Yeshua looked into the shining eyes of the preacher. Even before he was fully immersed in the eddying waters of the Jordan, Yeshua had decided. He would block his ears to the siren call of tempting normality. He would remain in the wilderness. He would become a disciple of John the Baptist.

And so it was that Yeshua dwelt in the wilderness listening to John teach about the kingdom of God, about the Holy Spirit, about how you could be baptized by the Holy Spirit, about God's desire for souls to bear fruit. And what all that meant.

And Yeshua did the processes for spiritual development which John taught and guided.

Some disciples could not sustain their confrontation with the wilderness. They left and returned to structures and tokens. As Yeshua watches them go, he understands why they leave. The wilderness is hard. The temptation is ever-present to leave the narrow path which seemingly has no end and return to normality.

Yeshua re-focuses. He commits. Whatever John asks of him, he does.

There are carrots along the path: spiritual visions and feelings of ineffable peace.

One day in the wilderness, during a spiritual process, the extraordinary manifests. It is the most stunning moment in Yeshua's life.

His soul is baptized by the Holy Spirit.

The Holy Spirit enters into him. He feels expanded beyond the boundaries of his physical body. And he hears inner words which he repeats out loud: "You are my son; today I have become your Father."

Yeshua may have entered into the wilderness as a normal man but he was normalized no longer.

> Yeshua revealed [beside the] Jordan the fullness
> of the Kingdom of Heaven, which existed before
> the totality. Moreover he was begotten as Son,
> moreover he was anointed, moreover he was
> atoned, moreover he atoned.
>
> - Gospel of Philip (88) [2]

After the baptism of his soul, Yeshua is taken aside by his teacher. The Baptist tells him that now Yeshua has a burden: he has the responsibility of giving others the same opportunity that he had been given. He has to stand ready to become a light for others. If anything is to happen to John, Yeshua is to take up ministry and take the message about the kingdom of God into the towns and villages.

---

[2] I have changed the phrase "Sovereignty of Heaven" to "Kingdom of Heaven" which is the phrase used in the Isenberg translation. See Appendices One and Two.

Yeshua consents but he cannot see that happening any time soon. John is wiry and tough. He'll live for decades. But John is not concerned for his physical health. He knows that his preaching will upset the hierarchy. It must upset them. It has upset them. He is preaching that the old Jewish law and the old way are not enough anymore. He is saying that everyone is spiritually equal. How can a religious hierarchy of priests swallow that? Accept that everyone is spiritually equal?

John preaches that the old covenant between man and God is no more. God wants more. The people cannot just obey the law and keep the Ten Commandments and expect all to be well. God wants them to step up to another level. He wants them to transform their souls and be baptized by the Holy Spirit and realize the kingdom of God. That spells the death of the hierarchy, the death of the entire machinery of the Jewish priesthood.

Soldiers come for John. He is arrested and thrown in prison. He has angered King Herod. Herod has been told that John was criticizing him for marrying his brother's wife. But the suspicion is that senior priests have been whispering in King Herod's ear, poisoning his mind against John. The priests did not like the following that John was getting. They did not want people to change their ways. They wanted them to keep on doing exactly what they had always done: keep the Law, tithe their incomes, donate to the Temple, make sacrifices, stay in their place, stay normal.

With the arrest of his teacher, Yeshua does what he had promised to do: he starts his ministry. He takes word of the kingdom of God into the villages and towns.

But Yeshua does not leave the wilderness behind.

Instead he takes the essence of the wilderness with him into the villages of Galilee. He seeks to disturb people out of their complacency, out of their sleep, out of their drunkenness with the things of the averaged world.

As John had done, he starts gathering disciples to him, the ones who get it, the ones who have a true hunger and thirst for the path. Yeshua has his own words but, in the end, there was nothing different between what Yeshua preached and what John had taught.

Of course, we now remember John's student not as "Yeshua" but by a Greek-then-Latinized version of his name.

Jesus.

> This is a colorized version of the black-and-white accounts found in the first three Gospels but I have not colored in outlines that aren't there. For the Biblical basis of this recounting of Jesus's journey with John the Baptist, see Appendix One.

John and Jesus

Years after Jesus's death, the Gospel writers fretted that Jesus going out into the wilderness to John the Baptist made Jesus look the lesser of the two spiritual figures.

There were four points from the oral tradition that the writer of the Gospel of Mark could not get around:

1. Jesus spent a substantial of time in the wilderness.
2. Jesus originally went into the wilderness to see John the Baptist.
3. Jesus was baptized in water by John the Baptist.
4. In his time with John the Baptist, Jesus experienced baptism by the Holy Spirit.

In order to minimize the importance of John's role in the emergence of Jesus, Mark minimized Jesus's time with John the Baptist – slashing it to a matter of minutes and then having Jesus wander off pointlessly into the wilderness.

The writers of the Gospels also put words into John's mouth indicating that all he was doing was preparing the way for one who would come later:

> "After me comes he who is mightier than I, the
> strap of whose sandals I am not worthy to stoop
> down and untie. I have baptized you with water,
> but he will baptize you with the Holy Spirit."
> - John the Baptist, Mark 1:7-8

One can see how a forced this passage is by considering that nowhere in any of the Gospels do we see a living Jesus actually baptize anyone with the Holy Spirit. In high contrast, Jesus is baptized by the Holy Spirit when he is under the charge of John.

Moreover, this passage admits that John understood baptism by the Holy Spirit *before he met Jesus*. How could he have understood it unless he himself had first-hand experience of it? Without such an experience how could he have vividly described it as being baptism by "fire"? (Matt 3:11; Luke 3:16)

Remarkably, the Gospel of Luke admits that the Holy Spirit filled John the Baptist before Jesus was – a long time before Jesus was – attributing it as having happened while John was still in his mother's womb (Luke 1:15). There is no way that Luke would have made such a concession unless floating around was the general acknowledgment that John had been baptized by the Holy Spirit before Jesus was.

Luke also admits that the so-called "Lord's Prayer" actually originated with John the Baptist:

> Now Jesus was praying in a certain place, and
> when he finished, one of his disciples said to him,
> "Lord, teach us to pray, as John taught his
> disciples." And he said to them, "When you pray,
> say: 'Father, hallowed be your name. Your
> kingdom come. Give us each day our daily bread,
> and forgive us our sins, for we ourselves forgive
> everyone who is indebted to us. And lead us not
> into temptation.'"
>
> - Luke 11:1-4

If the only time that Jesus spent with John the Baptist was a few minutes being baptized by water, how could he have learned and memorized the Lord's Prayer?

Most tellingly of all, this subservient role for John is never reflected in the recorded words of Jesus. Throughout his remaining time, Jesus would only ever say the most reverential things about his teacher – words which eloquently attest that Jesus knew John the Baptist far, far longer than a handful of minutes.[3] As you read what Jesus said about John, ask yourself: *Has anyone in the history of the world ever said such things about someone they knew for three-and-a-half minutes?*

> "Truly, I say to you, among those born of women
> there has arisen no one greater than John the
> Baptist."
>
> - Jesus, Matthew 11:11

There may be some dispute about who Jesus's father was: God? The Holy Spirit? Joseph? But there is no dispute that Jesus had an earthly mother and her name was Mary. In saying that no-one born

---

[3] That Jesus's preaching ministry starts only after his meeting with John the Baptist is independently attested in the Gospel of Mark, Gospel of John, Gospel of Thomas and Q. See Appendix Two.

of woman has arisen greater than John the Baptist, Jesus is rating John as equal to or above Jesus himself.

> Jesus said, "From Adam to John the Baptist, among those born of women, no one is so much greater than John the Baptist that his eyes should not be averted."
>
>   - Gospel of Thomas 46[4]

The most revered people in the Jewish religion were the prophets – Moses, Isaiah, Elijah, etc. Jesus describes John as not equal to these legendary prophets but as greater than them.

> "What then did you go out to see? A prophet? Yes, I tell you, and more than a prophet."
>
>   - Luke 7:26.

For Jesus, John the Baptist is the turning point from the prophets of old to something entirely new:

> "The Law and the Prophets were proclaimed until John. Since that time, the good news of the kingdom of God is being preached..."
>
>   - Jesus, Luke, 16:16 (NIV)

This is how important John was: John the Baptist was the turning point – not Jesus.

In the last days of his life, when he is challenged as to what gives him the authority to say the things he does, Jesus sets himself to appeal to the authority of John:

> And they came again to Jerusalem. And as he was walking in the temple, the chief priests and the scribes and the elders came to him, and they said

---

[4] See Appendix Two for a discussion of sources. As we shall see, a proper understanding of the teachings of Jesus makes this non-canonical Gospel of Thomas extremely coherent with the Gospels of Mark, Matthew and Luke.

to him, "By what authority are you doing these things, or who gave you this authority to do them?" Jesus said to them, "I will ask you one question; answer me, and I will tell you by what authority I do these things. Was the baptism of John from heaven or from man? Answer me." And they discussed it with one another, saying, "If we say, 'From heaven,' he will say, 'Why then did you not believe him?' But shall we say, 'From man'?"– they were afraid of the people, for they all held that John really was a prophet. So they answered Jesus, "We do not know." And Jesus said to them, "Neither will I tell you by what authority I do these things."

- Mark 11:27-33

And Jesus knew before he asked them that these scribes and chief priests and elders did not know. It was a trick question because there were actually two baptisms: one in water which was from man and one by the Holy Spirit which was from "heaven".

The Gospel of Mark is the earliest and the most reliable of the Biblical Gospels when it comes to events of the life of Jesus. It starts not with Jesus but with John, the voice of one crying in the wilderness.

John is the first person to mention "the kingdom of God". He is the first to refer to the "Holy Spirit" and baptism by the Holy Spirit (Mark 1:8; Matt 3:2,11; Luke 3:16).

The bizarre nativity stories of Matthew and Luke are, at least in part, stitched on the front to make Jesus look well and truly sanctified before he ever met John. The author of the Gospel of Luke is so disturbed by the pivotal role of John that he makes John into a cousin of Jesus (Luke 1:15).

Neither John nor Jesus was born special.

Jesus became special – very special – through the inner work he did under John's guidance. Decades after Jesus's death, the Gospels of Matthew and Luke and John were slanted to make it look as if Jesus had been born special.

He wasn't.

He was just an ordinary, probably illiterate construction worker who, through his devotion to inner spiritual work, became the most pivotal spiritual figure in human history.

And that is an infinitely more inspiring story than any tale of a virgin birth.

The new teachings of John/Jesus

"I will utter what has been hidden since the foundation of the world."
- Matthew 13:35

John the Baptist and Jesus both believed that they were preaching something entirely new... something that had been hidden since the dawn of time... something so radical that existing vocabulary could not encompass it. It is hard to overestimate how radical the preaching of John the Baptist was. He preached the path of inner, individual spiritual change. It was not the nation of Israel that had to change its ways and restore its relationship with God. It was each individual Israelite – one person at a time – who had to change: change their ways, change their heart, go beyond where they were now, and step up to a higher level.

The Israelites – the descendants of Abraham – believed that they had a covenant with God but, John says, "No. You have to go beyond that now. It's up to each individual to go on a spiritual path of inner change."

> "Well, then, start producing fruits in keeping with
> a change of heart, and don't even start saying to
> yourselves, 'We have Abraham for our father.'
> Let me tell you, God can raise up children for
> Abraham right out of these rocks."
>
>   - John the Baptist, Luke 3:85

In order to convey this new knowledge, John coined two new expressions: "the kingdom of God" and "the Holy Spirit".

The expression "the kingdom of God" does not appear in the Old Testament.

The phrase "holy spirit" is only used three times in the Old Testament and its usage there is different. John and then Jesus used the term "Holy Spirit" to refer to a distinct spiritual entity.

Another unique piece of Jesus-speak was "Son of Man". Surely that expression too originated with John the Baptist.

Why did John and Jesus need these entirely new expressions?

Because what they were trying to explain was new and radically different from anything Israelites had ever heard about before.

The kingdom of God

From day one of his preaching, Jesus emphasized that he was preaching for one reason only: to tell people about "the kingdom of God".

There seem to be three popular explanations among academics, theologians and the general populace of what he was referring to:

1. "The kingdom of God" was code referring to throwing off the yoke of Roman rule and re-establishing Jewish hegemony over the land. Israel is the land of God; the Jews are God's people;

---

[5] Translation from Robert J. Miller (ed), *The Complete Gospels*.

therefore, proclaiming the coming of "the kingdom of God" is declaration of a revolution of liberation from Rome.

2. "The kingdom of God" is "eschatological" in nature. "Eschatology" means "the study of the end". The "coming of the kingdom of God" refers to the end of this era and that God (or his representative) is coming to Earth to rule it... and/or to judge it... and/or to bring the world to an end in the Apocalypse... and/or herald the dawn of a New Age. (If this sounds vague, well, welcome to the wonderful world of eschatology.) This is now the standard academic position on Jesus. As this Brave New World never eventuated, Jesus was a deluded apocalyptic preacher.

3. "The kingdom of God" is some sort of reference to heaven and life after death.

But there is a fourth possibility:

4. "The kingdom of God" is a phrase invented by John the Baptist in order to help explain something in the path of inner spiritual growth.

The first three possibilities you will find expanded upon all over the place: in theological tomes, Sunday sermons, scholarly works, populist books and videos on YouTube.

The fourth possibility, you will struggle to find anything on. It is this possibility that will be explained and made sense of in this book. Because this possibility is the actuality.

Do you really think John the Baptist would have needed to invent new expressions to get across the idea of throwing off the yoke of Roman rule and re-establishing Jewish government?

Do you really think John the Baptist would have needed new expressions to promote the idea of an apocalypse? That's talked about in the Old Testament – see the Book of Daniel. No need for a new vocabulary to explain that.

Do you really think John the Baptist would have needed new expressions to get across the idea of dying and going to a life hereafter?

But John and Jesus did need new expressions to explain a mystical path of inner spiritual growth and emergence because that was something which the Israelite people had no existing parameters to understand.

The split ministry

Time and again, Jesus said that his mission is to preach "the kingdom of God". The Gospel of Matthew generally records this phrase as "the kingdom of heaven".

So difficult was this concept to convey that Jesus flatly declared that he would not even attempt to explain it to the masses. Just like John before him, he was only going to truly reveal the nature of the spiritual path to his inner sanctum of dedicated disciples. They were different. They were on a path of inner evolution that would enable them to realize what these expressions meant. They would have a chance to experience the Holy Spirit and realize the kingdom of God. To the general populace, he was only going to talk in parables. He was going to talk in code.

Like John before him, Jesus was on a fishing expedition. When he talked to the masses, he knew that the vast majority of men and women would never stay the long course of true inner spiritual evolution. He was fishing for those few people who would.

> "Listen! A sower went out to sow. And as he sowed, some seed fell along the path, and the birds came and devoured it. Other seed fell on

rocky ground, where it did not have much soil, and immediately it sprang up, since it had no depth of soil. And when the sun rose, it was scorched, and since it had no root, it withered away. Other seed fell among thorns, and the thorns grew up and choked it, and it yielded no grain. And other seeds fell into good soil and produced grain, growing up and increasing and yielding thirtyfold and sixtyfold and a hundredfold." And he said, "He who has ears to hear, let him hear."

- Mark 4:3-9

Only few in the audience would be the fertile deep soil. Only a handful would have a burning thirst for something more in life. These few would hunger and thirst enough to take up their cross, leave their lives behind and become disciples. These few would go through spiritual processes whereby the Holy Spirit could be experienced and not just be words fading in the air.

And here is the unfortunate reality for most academics and theologians: they don't understand that, for all their education and degrees, for all the admirable earnestness of their efforts, for all their books and undoubted intellect, for all my personal gratitude for their works and insights, they are ultimately in the exact same boat as those illiterate Israelites listening to Jesus: they have no experiential reference point to understand what John and Jesus meant by "the Holy Spirit", "the kingdom of God" and "baptism by the Holy Spirit".

They can hear but not understand.

Actually, these academics and theologians are in a leakier boat than those illiterate Israelite peasants because they are only getting fragments of Jesus's actual words.

We are going to embark on a quest that Jesus himself baulked at. He baulked at the task of explaining the kingdom of God to the masses. In this book, you will be given the opportunity to understand the meanings of "the kingdom of God", "the Holy Spirit", "baptism by the Holy Spirit" and "Son of Man".

Fortunately, I have an advantage that John and Jesus did not have. Science has given us insights into the hidden nature of reality – the vibrational reality that lies below solid objects. These breakthrough concepts actually make it easier to explain and understand the Holy Spirit and the kingdom of God.

I have another great advantage that John and Jesus did not have: I am able to draw upon the words of other mystics. John and Jesus thought that the spiritual emergences happening to them and their disciples were new in the history of humankind. After all, the Israelites were the chosen people of God; surely these new inner spiritual breakthroughs must signify something entirely new in the relationship between God and the Israelites. But the truth is that such spiritual emergences had already happened to other mystics in centuries gone by. And they would happen again after John and Jesus had departed this earthly plane.

Jesus the preacher

> And they went into Capernaum, and immediately on the Sabbath he entered the synagogue and was teaching. And they were astonished at his teaching, for he taught them as one who had authority, and not as the scribes.
>
> - Mark 1:21-22

The instant Jesus spoke to crowds something immediately distinguished him from other speakers: authority.

What makes you a genuine authority?

Reading books?

University degrees?

Calling yourself a consultant?

Writing a book?

There is only one thing: **Experience.**

You don't understand until you can stand on your experience. Until then you just have words and theories.

When Jesus talked, people immediately recognized that this was not just book learning. This was someone who knew, who understood, who had experience – someone for whom "the Holy Spirit" and "the kingdom of God" were not just words.

Jesus Delusion #1

Jesus was an anti-Roman revolutionary

Under this idea, the "kingdom of God" is interpreted as a theocratic kingdom on Earth, and Jesus was a Jewish revolutionary spruiking the overthrow of the Roman occupation and the establishment of a "kingdom of God" – an Israelite state which would be ruled by an Ayatollah-like religious leader on God's behalf. That ruler would (presumably) be Jesus.

In 2013, a book along these lines called *Zealot* came out. The author was Reza Aslan who combined his skills in creative writing with his religious studies to create an entertaining read. The logic of this book is straightforward:

- Jesus was crucified by the Romans
- The Romans wouldn't do this without a good reason. (Though the author gives accounts of Pilate crucifying thousands and paints Pontius Pilate as a despot who would not even bother looking at the name of a Jew who was down to be crucified.)
- Therefore, Jesus must have been a great danger to them.
- Therefore, he must have been a political rebel – a rebel preaching the coming of the kingdom of God. This was a revolutionary war cry to throw out the Romans and establish an independent Jewish state which would, de facto, be the kingdom of the Jewish God.
- All the Jewish listeners understood what Jesus was talking about when he referenced "the kingdom of God" – he was

referring to a new state, one not ruled by the Romans. It was a call to a politico-religious revolution.

This idea is by no means new. Indeed, it is arguably the oldest idea in the quest for the historical Jesus. It goes back to a German scholar Herman Reimarus in the 18th Century who wisely did not seek publication of this thesis during his lifetime. When he died in 1768, he left behind a mountain of papers that were gathered into a work called "Fragments" which ran to about 4,000 pages and were published posthumously in seven volumes. In it, he argued that Jesus was a political revolutionary but, after his death, his disciples did a right-hand turn and decided to found a religion in his name.

There is any number of criticisms or questions that can be raised about Aslan's version of Reimarus's thesis. Amazingly, Aslan contradicts one of Jesus's clearest statements about the kingdom of God: that the average listener wouldn't understand it.

> "...for those outside everything is in parables, so that they may indeed see but not perceive, and may indeed hear but not understand..."
> - Mark 4:11-12

Aslan says: No, no. *They all understood it perfectly.*

> "The Kingdom of God is a call to revolution, plain and simple." (p. 136)
> "... 'The Kingdom of God' – a term that would have been understood by Jew and gentile alike as implying revolt against Rome..." (p. 20)

Then Aslan claims that, in order to protect himself from immediate arrest, Jesus "...consciously chose to veil the Kingdom of God in abstruse and enigmatic parables that are nearly impossible to understand." (p. 141)

You cannot have it both ways. You cannot, on one hand, claim that everybody immediately understood what the "kingdom of God" meant; and then, on the other hand, say that Jesus used parables to obscure its meaning (a meaning which everybody already understood!).

(By the way, as you read this present book, you will come to understand each and every one of these parables that are "nearly impossible to understand".)

Not entirely dissimilar is the idea that John the Baptist and Jesus were both apocalyptic preachers proclaiming the coming of an "eschaton" – an end-of-days scenario where God (and/or his representative) would descend and establish a new age on Earth. Under this interpretation, the "kingdom of God" is a kingdom that will be established on earth by divine forces (rather than a violent human revolution) and would be ruled by God or his messianic representative. This is now the received academic view of Jesus's teachings.

Both Alsan's political decoding and the apocalyptic decoding of "the kingdom of God" flounder because:

1. They totally fail to explain WHY John the Baptist felt it necessary to come up with totally new expressions. Why didn't he just use current, well-understood terms?

2. They totally ignore the other crucial coinage of John the Baptist: "the Holy Spirit". They do not even try to decode what that means or what "baptism by the Holy Spirit" refers to.

3. They cannot explain why Jesus talked in parables. It is not hard to understand a new political kingdom or an apocalypse. So why did he speak in parables?

4. Moreover, they cannot explain what those parables mean – how can a political or earthly kingdom be like a mustard seed (Mark 4:30-32)? Or like yeast-in-bread (Matthew 13:33)? What value does a decoding of "the kingdom of God" have if it does not shed any light on Jesus's parables?

There is an additional annoyance with the academic apocalypticist view of Jesus:

5. They never attempt to explain why Jesus was an apocalypticist. The standard "explanation" is: Well, there were a few Jewish apocalypticists around at the time. This is the equivalent of explaining why someone became a serial killer by saying "There were a few of them around at the time." That is not a proper explanation; it's just a grouping. If Jesus believed in a forthcoming apocalypse, why did he believe it? What did it have to do with the Holy Spirit and baptism by the Holy Spirit? What did it have to do with the parables he taught?

This is not to say that Jesus never said anything apocalyptic. This book will reveal that Jesus was, first and foremost, a spiritual teacher teaching the inner path of transformation of the soul – anything apocalyptic he may have said derived from that.

Jesus's references to a forthcoming apocalypse will be discussed and explained in the sequel to this book, *The Crucifixion Code*.

The Bible is the infallible Word of God

The Bible is a mess.

Have you actually read the Bible from cover to cover?

It's a mess.

Jesus's teachings obviously contradict the teachings in the Old Testament. They cannot both be true. The Old Testament reads: "An eye for an eye; a tooth for a tooth." That is not what Jesus taught. He taught "turn the other cheek".

Even just the four Biblical Gospels are a mess. There are contradictions and anomalies everywhere. To name just one: The Gospel of Mark has Jesus executed on the day of the Passover; the Gospel of John has him executed on the day before the Passover. They simply both cannot be true. They cannot both be the infallible word of God. One of them has to go. As soon as you admit even one example of fallibility then everything is up for grabs.´

Moreover, the decision to include those four early Christian writings (the four Gospels) in the New Testament and exclude other writings was a decision taken by fallible men. It excluded other significant early Christian writings. Certainly, there are grounds for thinking that the Gospel of John should not have been included. It is just so different from the other three Gospels.

As we shall see in the course of this book, the Gospel of Thomas (not included in the Bible) is much more coherent with the first three Gospels than the Gospel of John. I will be citing the Gospel of Thomas often. (See Appendix Two to learn more about the Gospel of Thomas and other sources cited in this book.)

If you think God was guiding every translation (from Aramaic to Greek, from Greek to Latin, from Latin to English), get real.

(No, seriously, please come back to the real world.)

If you think that God was guiding every copying of text, every stroke of the pen of every trained and untrained scribe, take a look at Bart D. Ehrman's *Misquoting Jesus*, a highly readable overview of how textual errors could and did creep in.

If you think that God guided the Church authorities in their selection of what to put into the New Testament... Seriously? Scholars now agree that only seven of Paul's epistles can definitively be attributed to him. Others are dubious; or even obvious forgeries.

And what is the Book of Revelation doing in there?

(See Appendix Two for an overview of the sources I have drawn on and why.)

Jesus Delusion #3

Jesus's ministry was all about healing and miracles

Because they cannot understand Jesus's teachings about the kingdom of God, many Christian preachers focus instead on the miraculous healings that the Biblical Gospels ascribe to Jesus. These prove Jesus's divinity and power.

One thing we can be sure of is that Jesus did not want to be known as a healer. On several occasions, he basically says: "Okay I'll heal you but don't tell anyone." Nevertheless, the person goes and blabs (Mark 1:40-44, 5:35-43, 7:32-36, 8:22-26). Obviously, this is not what Jesus wanted to be known for. It was not what he saw his ministry as being about. Yet a lot of Jesus's initial fame may have come from these healings and the casting out of demons.

In Jesus's time, there was no knowledge of germs, how the brain worked, hysterical illnesses, psychosomatic complaints, mental illnesses... so such things were put down to "demons". If someone had had an epileptic seizure, it was thought they were possessed by a demon. If someone was paranoid or schizophrenic, they were possessed. As such, people back then were much more open to the power of suggestion. Jesus was not the only traveling healer and exorcist of demons. Jesus seems to have been distinguished by doing "healings" for free – and, seemingly, by being reluctant to do them.

This was also a time when there was a conflation of illness with sinning: you would not have got sick in the first place if you hadn't done something spiritually wrong. As such, forgiveness of sins and healing people are muddled together in tales of Jesus's miracles.

Jesus himself suggests that his power to help the suffering came from people's image of him and the power of suggestion:

> Jesus said, "No prophet is welcome on his home turf; doctors don't cure those who know them."
> - Gospel of Thomas, 31.

Or, as it is recounted in the Gospel of Mark (6:1-6):

> He went away from there and came to his hometown, and his disciples followed him. And on the Sabbath he began to teach in the synagogue, and many who heard him were astonished, saying, "Where did this man get these things? What is the wisdom given to him? How are such mighty works done by his hands? Is not this the carpenter, the son of Mary and brother of James and Joses and Judas and Simon? And are not his sisters here with us?" And they took offense at him. And Jesus said to them, "A prophet is not without honor, except in his hometown and among his relatives and in his own household." And he could do no mighty work there, except that he laid his hands on a few sick people and healed them. And he marveled because of their unbelief.

So healings don't just come from the power or authority of Jesus. It depends on the person's state of mind.

Interestingly, in the Gospel of Mark (3:14-15), when Jesus calls together the Twelve to send them out as emissaries, he tells them to go out and proclaim the message of the kingdom of God and he gives them power to cast out demons – but gives no instructions for them to heal.

There are Christian "healing ministries" today. The most famous is the Benny Hinn ministry (www.bennyhinn.org). His "Christian Miracle Healing Crusades" attract thousands of people to packed-out stadiums. A number of investigations have failed to detect even one case of a cure. Of course, there may be temporary elation caused by adrenalin and the placebo effect.

Jesus was focused on preaching the kingdom of God. All else was peripheral to that. Faith-based Christian preachers who do not make that the center of their ministry are not in alignment with Jesus. But how could they be when they do not understand what Jesus meant by "the kingdom of God"?

Part II

The kingdom of God

"Thy kingdom come."

- Luke 11:2 (ERE)

Preaching the kingdom of God

"I must preach the good news of the kingdom of
God to the other towns as well; for I was sent for
this purpose."

- Luke 4:43.

That's it.

That's Jesus's whole preaching mission summed up in his own
words: preaching about the kingdom of God.

And when he was demanded of the Pharisees,
when the kingdom of God should come, he
answered them and said, The kingdom of God
cometh not with observation:
Neither shall they say, Lo here! or, lo there! for,
behold, the kingdom of God is within you.[6]

- Luke:17: 20-21 (KJV)

Note carefully: *within you.*

Not of this world. *Within you.*

Not something that can be observed with earthly eyes.

Within you.

Not a post-revolutionary Israel that will exist once the Romans
are kicked out.

Within you.

Not a place up in the sky that you go to once you're dead.

Within you.

Not something that Church leaders hold the keys to.

Within you.

---

[6] An alternative translation is in your midst: "...for behold, the kingdom of God is
in the midst of you." (ESV). As we shall later see, this translation is even more in
line with the mystic idea of the Holy Spirit being a pervasive field that is both
inside you and outside you.

The Mystic Path

Jesus said, "I will give you what no eye has seen,
what no ear has heard, what no hand has touched,
what has not arisen in the human heart."
- Gospel of Thomas, 17

The true mystic path is the path of inner spiritual evolution in this lifetime.

Not the ascension of your soul to heaven when you die.

The evolution of your soul while you are alive.

The Holy Spirit

An unbelievable number of words have been written misinterpreting John the Baptist's expression "the kingdom of God". By comparison, there has been amazingly scant attention paid to another coinage of John the Baptist: "the Holy Spirit". Yet it is absolutely pivotal in Jesus's journey and his teachings. Even before Jesus makes an entrance on the scene, John the Baptist flags that his mission will be all about baptism by the Holy Spirit:

"...he will baptize you with the Holy Spirit."
- Mark 1:8

What Jesus experienced in his time with John the Baptist was not "baptism by God"; it was "baptism by the Holy Spirit".

In those days Jesus came from Nazareth of Galilee
and was baptized by John in the Jordan. And when
he came up out of the water, immediately he saw
the heavens being torn open and the Spirit
descending on him like a dove. And a voice came
from heaven, "You are my beloved Son; with you
I am well pleased."
- Mark 1:9-11

The earliest versions of the Gospel of Luke have this voice-from-beyond tag Jesus as having become a Son *on that exact day* – and not prior:

> "You are my son; today I have become your father."
>
> - Luke 3:22[7]

No wonder later scribes changed this passage to something more digestible for faith-based Christians such that modern Bibles render this passage as: "You are my beloved Son; with you I am well pleased."

Fragments of the Gospel of the Hebrews survive only due to critiques of it by early Church Fathers such as Jerome. In two of these fragments, Jesus is specifically tagged as being a Son of the Holy Spirit:

> And it happened that when the Lord came up out of the water, the whole fountain of the holy spirit came down on him and rested on him. It said to him "My Son, I was waiting for you in all the prophets, waiting for you to come so I could rest in you..."
> Just now my mother, the holy spirit, took me.[8]

Similarly, there is an apparent reference to the Holy Spirit as the mother of Jesus in the Gospel of Thomas (101) where Jesus says, "...my true mother gave me life".

Even in the Biblical Gospels, Jesus's status as being a son of the Holy Spirit is specifically recognized: Mary, the mother of Jesus, is

---

[7] Translation from Robert J. Miller (ed), *The Complete Gospels*, p. 125.
[8] Robert J. Miller (ed), *The Complete Gospels*, pp. 431, 432.

not said to be impregnated by God but *impregnated by the Holy Spirit* (Matt 1:18; Luke 1:36).

According to Jesus, what is the greatest gift that God can give man?

The Holy Spirit.

> "If you then, who are evil, know how to give good gifts to your children, how much more will the heavenly Father give the Holy Spirit to those who ask him!"
>
> > - Luke 11:13

The key to entering the kingdom of God is to be born again with the Holy Spirit:

> Nicodemus said to him, "How can a man be born when he is old? Can he enter a second time into his mother's womb and be born?"
> Jesus answered, "Truly, truly, I say to you, unless one is born of water and the Spirit, he cannot enter the kingdom of God."
>
> > - John 3:4-5

Jesus is deeply protective of the Holy Spirit:

> "Truly, I say to you, all sins will be forgiven the children of man, and whatever blasphemies they utter, but whoever blasphemes against the Holy Spirit never has forgiveness, but is guilty of an eternal sin"
>
> > - Mark 3:28-29[9]

Think about the implications of this extraordinary passage: it is the Holy Spirit that is the most sacrosanct, the most pure, the one

---

[9] There are similar passages in Matthew 12:32, Luke 12:10 and the Gospel of Thomas 44.

thing about which a bad word should not be uttered. Badmouth God the Father, that's forgivable. But don't say one bad word about the Holy Spirit. It is more sacrosanct than God.

Tellingly, in none of the synoptic Gospels (Mark, Matthew, Luke) do the words "I am the Son of God" come out of Jesus's mouth. We are inexorably led towards this conclusion: for the last two thousand years, Jesus should never have been described as "the Son of God" but as "Son of the Holy Spirit".

So what is this "Holy Spirit" thing?

The "Holy Spirit" is referred to by other names by other mystics.

In the third century A.D., Plotinus referred to it as "the One".

Centuries prior to Jesus, the multiple writers of the great Indian mystic texts, *The Upanishads*, referred to it variously as "Brahman" (Great Cosmic Spirit), "the Lord of Love", "the Self" and, indeed, occasionally, "the One".[10]

So what is this thing with many names?

The Parable of the Signal

There is a Wi-Fi signal that goes throughout the entire universe. It is powerful and uniform.

As it is universal, it runs through every computer. Every computer picks up this signal but it doesn't show up on the computer display, so people using computers don't even know it exists. But, very occasionally, a computer operator really searches their computer hard and finds the signal. It's small. It's a flicker. The person at the computer has no idea it is a universal signal going

---

[10] For example, it is referred to as "the One" in the Mundaka Upanishad II, 2:5-6. p.114. and the Taittiriya Upanishad I, 4:3 p.139.

throughout the universe. They just think it is a tiny flicker of energy unique to this particular computer and just contained within it.

On rare occasions, other computer operators discover this flicker of energy and they all conclude the same thing: *Oh, it's an independent flicker of pure energy unique to this computer.*

But, in the course of time, one particularly determined computer operator realizes that there are bugs in the computer. They do not know where the bugs came from but they are sure that the computer has flaws that can be cleared up. So they work and work on the computer, debugging it, and, as they do so, the signal starts to get stronger. Via this signal, the computer begins to receive flashes, images, visions.

They continue to work on getting the bugs out of the computer. Eventually they work on it long enough that something happens that is startling and totally unexpected. The computer is so de-bugged that it totally and permanently locks onto the Wi-Fi signal. In fact, it fuses with the signal, and it can never again be separated from the signal.

The computer operator comes to realize that this Wi-Fi signal shouldn't be thought of as a signal but as a field. A field that runs through the entire universe.

They also discover that, out there somewhere, also connected to this Wi-Fi field, is the father of all computers – a massive SuperComputer of unbelievable and unearthly power. Now that this little insignificant computer has fused with this universal field, this SuperComputer can potentially connect to it.

And the computer operator sets out to teach others about this...

Best explanation of the Holy Spirit ever:

Just as physical entities – rocks, planets, suns, human bodies - exist in and on space-time so too do spiritual entities (God and souls) exist in and on the Holy-Spirit/The-One/Brahman.

> ... God's ground and the soul's ground are one ground.
>
> - Meister Eckhart, *Complete Mystical Works of Meister Eckhart*, Sermon 51, p.273.

Ancient mystics on the Holy Spirit

The ancient mystics had a poorer vocabulary, no knowledge of vibrations or fields and fewer images to convey spiritual realities. Nevertheless, they took an almighty swing at explaining how this universal One/Brahman/Lord-of-Love/Holy-Spirit existed inside and through souls and throughout the spiritual universe.

> The Holy Spirit is in the revealed, she is below,
> she is in the hidden, she is above.
>
> - Gospel of Philip, 37.

> The Lord of Love is before and behind.
> He extends to the right and to the left.
> He extends above; he extends below.
>
> - Mundaka Upanishad II, 2:12, p.115.

> Like oil in sesame seeds, like butter In cream, like
> water in springs, like fire In firesticks, so dwells
> the Lord of Love, The Self, in the very depths of
> consciousness...
> The Self is hidden in the hearts of all, As butter
> lies hidden in cream.
>
> - Shvetashvatara Upanishad, I:15-16, p.219.

The Self, small as the thumb, dwelling in the
heart,
Be like the sun shining in the sky...
It may appear smaller than a hair's breadth.
But know the Self to be infinite.

- Shvetashvatara Upanishad, V:8-9,
p.229.

The Holy Spirit and the kingdom of God

His disciples said to him, "When will the kingdom
come?"
"It will not come by watching for it. It will not be
said, 'Look, here!' or 'Look, there!' Rather, the
Father's kingdom is spread out upon the earth,
and people don't see it."

- Gospel of Thomas, 113

Jesus and John the Baptist did not just talk about "the Holy
Spirit". They also talked about "the kingdom of God".

What is the relationship between these two?

There are differences in what these terms refer to but, for now,
I will treat them as identical as this will help you in the early part of
your journey to understanding. Later, I will explain the difference
and why Jesus and John the Baptist often favored the term "the
kingdom of God" or "the kingdom of heaven". Meanwhile, here is a
clue about the difference: when a soul is baptized by the Holy Spirit,
it enters into the kingdom of God:

"Truly, truly, I say to you, unless one is born of
water and the Spirit, he cannot enter the kingdom
of God."

- John 3:5

The kingdom of God/heaven

"...the (Father's) kingdom is within you and it is outside you..."

- Gospel of Thomas, 3

This spiritual field – the One, the Holy Spirit, Brahman – is vast. It is the spiritual universe on which God and the souls exist. But the soul, if it is aware of it at all, sees it only through a glass darkly. When the sun is eclipsed by the moon, you can only see a tiny fraction of the rays of the Sun – yet the Sun is vast. In a similar way, the traumatized energies of an untransformed soul block the perception of the vast energy of the Holy Spirit – reducing perception of it to a sliver, a speck.

From the soul's point of view, the "kingdom of heaven is like treasure hidden in a field..." (Matt 13:44). Hidden it may be, small it may be, but it has a value beyond everything else.

> Again, the kingdom of heaven is like a merchant in search of fine pearls, who, on finding one pearl of great value, went and sold all that he had and bought it.
>
> - Matthew 13:45-46.

From the point of view of an unevolved soul, the One/Brahman/Holy-Spirit/the-kingdom-of-God is hidden, it is distant, it is underneath, it is tiny. It is a small hidden seed – but it has the potential to "grow" within the soul. As we shall see, it gets larger in the soul via the purification/detraumatization of the soul.

The Upanishads sometimes use the term "the Self" to designate this seeming speck of the holy within oneself.

> That thumb-sized being enshrined in the heart...
> Is the Self indeed.
>
> - Katha Upanishad I, 1:12, p.92.

Each of us has this seemingly tiny sliver of the Self deep inside us. But all these seemingly separate Selfs turn out to be only one:

> There is only one Self in all creatures,
> The One appears many, just as the moon Appears
> many, reflected in water.
>
> - Amritabindu Upanishad 12, p.244.

But – and this is the big theme of *The Upanishads* – this "Self" which seems so tiny within us is actually Brahman, the cosmic spirit, the cosmic field, the Holy Spirit. In the words of a more modern seeker:

> What he (man) experiences in his inmost being, as
> spirit, is the universal Spirit.
>
> - Rudolf Steiner, *Christianity as Mystic Fact*, Chapter XII.

Likewise, for John the Baptist and Jesus, the tiny speck of the kingdom of God within you can grow large:

> And he said, "With what can we compare the kingdom of God, or what parable shall we use for it? It is like a grain of mustard seed, which, when sown on the ground, is the smallest of all the seeds on earth, yet when it is sown it grows up and becomes larger than all the garden plants and puts out large branches, so that the birds of the air can make nests in its shade."
>
> - Mark 4:30-32

The Chandogya Upanishad uses a stunningly similar analogy:

> Smaller than a grain of rice, smaller than a grain of barley, smaller than a mustard seed, smaller than a grain of millet, smaller even than the kernel of a grain of millet is the Self. This is the Self

dwelling in my heart, greater than the earth,
greater than the sky, greater than all the worlds.
- Chandogya Upanishad III, 14:3, pp.177-8.

Jesus provides perhaps the best analogy of all the ancient mystics:

"The kingdom of heaven is like yeast that a woman took and mixed with three measures of flour until all of it was leavened."
- Matthew 13:33 (ISV)

From the undeveloped soul's point of view, the "kingdom of God" currently appears tiny, small, distant – a fleck, a grain, a tiny scattering of yeast. Virtually undetectable. But, like yeast mixed with flour, it has massive potential. If the flour of the soul and the yeast of the Holy Spirit come together then both will be altered to create something better and greater. This is baptism by the Holy Spirit. That was what Jesus experienced in his time with John. It is the fusion of the soul with Spirit.

The coming of the kingdom of God

"...the kingdom of God has come upon you."
- Matthew 12:28.

The kingdom of God is not coming in the future. It has come. It has come within the souls of Jesus and John and doubtless other disciples of John the Baptist. And this meant it could also "come" – emerge – within the soul of any person.

But how? How can the kingdom of God "come" – grow within a soul and transform it?

51

Is there anywhere that Jesus explains the steps you need to go through in order to experience baptism by the Holy Spirit and so realize the kingdom of God?

Yes there is.

And it's been hiding in plain sight for two thousand years.

Jesus was born the Son of God

The Jesus of faith-based traditional Christianity never did any inner spiritual work. He never needed to be baptized by the Holy Spirit. He never needed to go on a spiritual journey to realize the kingdom of God inside his soul. He was already born the Son of God. Indeed, in the Gospel of John, Jesus was already the Son of God before Mary gave birth to him.

Ancient mythology is filled with tales of the sons of gods. It was not an idea unique to Jesus. Hercules was said to be the son of a mortal woman and Jupiter - likewise, Achilles.

The Roman Emperors would sometimes lay claim to be sons of Gods. Or they would be feted as such.

But, of course, Jesus was really unique.

- Prior to his birth, an angelic figure announced to the mother that her son would be born divine.
- The birth was ushered in with wondrous signs.
- He became a wandering preacher, telling people not to focus on material things but on spiritual matters.
- He performed miracles.
- He gathered disciples.
- He angered the powerful who dragged him before the Roman authorities.
- After his death, his followers swore that he still appeared to them.

This sounds like a summary of Jesus's life according to the Gospels of Matthew and Luke; but it is also a summary of stories told about a neo-Pythagorean philosopher called Apollonius of Tyana – except Apollonius worshipped pagan gods. He even lived in the same time of Jesus.[11] Neither of them knew about the other but subsequently their followers would debate between each other about who was the greater.

With all these sons-of-gods going around the Mediterranean, you can understand why later writers of the Gospels (Matthew and Luke and John) were keen to slot in material to make Jesus look like he was born a demi-God.

But there is none of the miraculous birth stuff in the earliest written of the Gospels, the Gospel of Mark, which starts off with John the Baptist preaching in the wilderness.

The Gospels are also concerned to make the case that Jesus was the Jewish "Messiah", supposedly foretold in prophecy, who would be born to be the savior of Israel. Ironically, these two campaigns get in each other's way. To make the case that Jesus was the Messiah, the Gospels have to make the case that Jesus was a descendant of King David. Accordingly, both Luke and Matthew have genealogies showing that Jesus's father, Joseph, was descended from King David (Matt 1:1-16; Luke 4:23-28). (Note that these two genealogies are wildly different.) But then they say that Jesus was not the son of Joseph but of the Holy Spirit (Matt 1:18; Luke 1:34-37) thereby destroying any genetic claim that Jesus could be the Jewish Messiah.

---

[11] There is a good discussion of Apollonius in the first chapter of Bart D. Ehrman, *How Jesus Became God: The Exaltation of a Jewish Preacher from Galilee.* Also see *Philostratus, The Life of Apollonius.* The F.C. Conybeare translation is available free online at http://www.livius.org/ap-ark/apollonius/life/va_00.html

Consider the claim that Jesus was born the "Son of God" in terms of recorded events in Jesus's adult life...

If Jesus was born divine - already possessed of all spiritual knowledge - why did he sit on his hands and do nothing for year after year? Why did he wait until he was around 30 years old to start teaching? There is a huge gap in the Gospels from Jesus at the age of twelve when, according to the Gospel of Luke (2:41-51), he debated with senior scribes in the Temple until some eighteen years later when he finally started preaching. Why did he waste that unconscionable amount of time doing construction work when he could have been out there educating people about the kingdom of God? But no, he doesn't start preaching until after spending time with John the Baptist and John's arrest.

If Jesus was born already spiritually transcendent, why did he seek out John at all?

Why do the Testaments record two spiritual transformations of the adult Jesus: the entry of the Holy Spirit (in his time with John) and the Transfiguration (Mark 9:1-8)? Why did Jesus need two transformations if he was already born the Son of God?

Why, in the oldest versions of Luke, is it recorded that, with the descent of the Holy Spirit, Jesus hears the words: "You are my son; today I have become your Father." (Luke 3:22)? How could that day have been the day that he became the Son if he was already born that way?

No wonder later copyists altered this sentence to make it less doctrinally distressing.

Why does Jesus praise John the Baptist as the originator of the teaching of the kingdom of God? (Luke 16:16)

If Jesus was miraculously born, why were his family shocked by his becoming a spiritual leader? And why did they set out to stage an intervention?

> When his family heard it, they went out to seize him, for people were saying, "He has gone out of his mind".
> - Mark 3:21

His family was more shocked by this change in Jesus than anyone else was. What the hell has happened to Jesus? Has he fallen under the spell of that cult of John the Baptist? Does he now think he is a guru or something?

The mother and brothers arrive to find they couldn't even get to Jesus to stage their intervention because he was surrounded by a crowd listening to him talk about the Holy Spirit.

> And his mother and his brothers came, and standing outside they sent to him and called him. And a crowd was sitting around him, and they said to him, "Your mother and your brothers are outside, seeking you."
> - Mark 3:31-32

Jesus probably thought to himself the equivalent: "Oh crap. This is not the time to deal with their concerns and shock."

> And he answered them, "Who are my mother and my brothers?" And looking about at those who sat around him, he said, "Here are my mother and my brothers! For whoever does the will of God, he is my brother and sister and mother."
> - Mark 3:33-35

Moreover, this is the only appearance by Jesus's mother in the entire Gospel of Mark. If a tiny fraction of the nativity stories in

Matthew and Luke were true, do you think his family would have been shocked and trying to intervene? Mary would have been like: "I always knew he was destined for this. I remember the angels and the wise men." But, no, she and his brothers were like: "*What the hell's happened to Yeshua?*"

And here is a deep lesson for anyone who sets out on the true path of spiritual inner evolution: it can cost you friends. You may have to go against what was taught to you by your parents or "authorities".

Jesus was not born special. He was not born the Son of God. He was an Average Jo who made himself special by the deep inner work he did. His persistence in this inner path led to baptism by the Holy Spirit. And that is truly inspirational.

But what was the path that this human Jesus trod in order to be baptized by the Holy Spirit? Did he ever reveal the inner path which a seeker needs to tread in order to realize the kingdom of God inside one's soul?

Yes he did.

And it's been hiding in plain sight for two thousand years...

Part III

The Beatitudes Code

"Are you... the Son of the Blessed One?"

- Mark 14:61

The Beatitudes

"Blessed are the poor in spirit, for theirs is the kingdom of heaven.

Blessed are those who mourn, for they will be comforted.

Blessed are the meek, for they will inherit the earth.

Blessed are those who hunger and thirst for righteousness, for they will be filled.

Blessed are the merciful, for they will be shown mercy.

Blessed are the pure in heart, for they will see God.

Blessed are the peace-makers, for they will be called children of God.

Blessed are those who are persecuted because of righteousness, for theirs is the kingdom of heaven.

Blessed are you when people insult you, persecute you and falsely say all kinds of evil against you because of me. Rejoice and be glad, because great is your reward in heaven, for in the same way they persecuted the prophets who were before you."

- Jesus, Matthew 5:3-11 (NIV)

Blessed

The Beatitudes (Matt 5:3-12) are the nine aphorisms of Jesus which start off "*Blessed are...*" For example: "Blessed are the merciful for they shall obtain mercy."

Jesus made a strict distinction between what he was prepared to teach in public and what he taught in private to his disciples. In public, he taught in parables.

The Beatitudes are not parables. That, in itself, should tell you a lot.

The almost universal perception among Christians – and others – is that the Beatitudes is the start of one of the most inspiring public speeches ever made: The Sermon on the Mount. The Beatitudes were proclaimed by Jesus, standing on a mount, before a great crowd of people – instructing them on how they should conduct their lives and the unexpected rewards that then would come their way. You can see this scene portrayed in many paintings and in films.

Except that the actual Gospel of Matthew says nothing like this. Instead, it clearly states that the Beatitudes were given as a private lecture to his disciples:

> Seeing the crowds, he went up on the mountain, and when he sat down, his disciples came to him. And he opened his mouth and taught them, saying...
>
> - Matthew 5:1-2.

Jesus wasn't even standing.

Jesus took his disciples away from the crowds so he could privately instruct them.

In the Bible, mountains signify the receiving of something from the divine. The Ten Commandments came down from a mountain (Exodus 19-20). It is on a mountain that Jesus would be Transfigured (Mark 9:2). It is from a mountain that Jesus gives authority to the Twelve Apostles to go out and preach the kingdom of God and cast out demons (Mark 3:13-17). And it is on a mountain that Jesus imparts the Beatitudes. This is a flashing-beacon signal that this is divine, high-level knowledge.

Clearly, this was not some public-access information broadcast. Rather, Jesus is giving select spiritual instruction to his inner sanctum. Indeed, the ninth and last Beatitude is obviously only directed at those disciples who would be going out and spreading his teachings. Instead of starting off with "Blessed are the", it starts off with "Blessed are you".

> "Blessed are you when others revile you and persecute you and utter all kinds of evil against you falsely on my account. Rejoice and be glad, for your reward is great in heaven, for so they persecuted the prophets who were before you."
> - Matthew 5:10-11

Moreover, as a guidebook to everyday living, the Beatitudes make no sense. How is it that the meek will inherit the earth? The earth belonged to conquerors like Alexander the Great and the Romans. Nothing meek about them. The merciful shall obtain mercy? Like that worked for Jesus when he was crucified and all the other Christian martyrs who were to come.

The Beatitudes were never taught by Jesus to the masses as a guidebook for everyday living – and they were never meant to be thought of like that. Rather, it was a secret teaching about the path of blessedness. Something is "blessed" if it is infused with holiness, the divine, spiritual redemption or divine will. Jesus was providing a road map to the path of being infused with the divine – with the Holy Spirit. This is what happened to Jesus himself in his time with John the Baptist. He was infused with the divine – baptized by the Holy Spirit.

The Beatitudes are a step-by-step guide to being baptized by the Holy Spirit. This makes the Beatitudes the most important teaching in the Gospels... indeed, in the whole Bible... indeed I believe it is the single most important teaching of all time.

And it has been hiding in plain sight for two thousand years.

I am at a loss to find anything that comes remotely close to the Beatitudes as containing so much spiritual guidance in so few words.

Jesus starts by referencing the ultimate goal all the disciples had: to experience baptism by the Holy Spirit and so enter their soul into the kingdom of God – or, as it is usually referred to in the Gospel of Matthew, "the kingdom of heaven".

"Blessed are the poor in spirit, for theirs is the kingdom of heaven."

This is the dramatic start which would have galvanized the disciples' attention.

Remember that these are the same disciples to whom the kingdom of God is revealed while the general public only receives cryptic parables (Mark 4:11-12). Jesus headlines this private talk by telling his disciples it is going to be about how to obtain to the kingdom of heaven/God. It does not get any more important than this.

Jesus starts with a shocking idea: that the kingdom of heaven won't be achieved by people rich in spirit but by those "poor in spirit" – those who are low or lowly, downcast or depressed, dejected or dispirited. Such are the people who will enter on the path. Jesus then outlines the six steps that being "poor in spirit" can lead to – the six steps that can take someone to "the kingdom of heaven" (baptism by the Holy Spirit).

As you read these steps, understand that Jesus is talking from direct experience: these are the stages he went through on his path of spiritual growth. They are also the stages that anyone – then and now – has to go through to truly evolve – psychologically, emotionally, spiritually evolve.

1. "Blessed are those who mourn..."

This is the first step on the path of blessedness: sadness, discomfort, inner discontent, regret, misery, depression... mourning.

If you are happy and carefree, why and how would you ever be motivated to do deep inner work – to heal, to evolve?

So the very first step on the path to blessedness is to be confronted by the spectre of meaninglessness... by inner discontent, sadness, anxiety, regret, frustration, depression.

Confucius put it succinctly: "No vexation, no enlightenment; no anxiety, no illumination." (Analects 7:8)

Jesus's use of the term "mourn" takes the insight of Confucius to another level. To truly start on this first step, you have to not just be "poor in spirit"; you have to **mourn**. When you mourn, you may be vexed and anxious and suffering and poor in spirit but there is an added dimension to mourning: **there is a sense of loss or void**... that something vital to feeling alive and happy is missing... your life is not how it is supposed to be... you pine to fill an emptiness... you ache to fill that gaping maw of meaninglessness... there is an unshakable sense that where there should be meaningfulness, there is an ache of meaninglessness.

When you mourn, you don't just suffer; *you ache for meaningfulness*. You ache to fill the black hole.

It was this sense of void that started me on the path of deep inner work. When I was twenty-nine, I was gripped by one pervasive, looping thought: *"There HAS to be more to life than this."*

It is important not to conflate mourning with grief. Grief is one type of mourning: you had something and you lost it and you grieve for its loss. This could be the loss of someone you loved or a job you loved or a dog you loved. But you can also mourn for something you never had. You can mourn that you never received love and acceptance from your parents. You can mourn that you never found a life partner to build a life with. You can mourn that you never had a chance to have a great career. You can mourn that you never had a fit, healthy body. You can mourn for things you never had... as well as for things you had and lost...

Whether two thousand years ago or right now, it is mourning that starts people off on deep inner growth work: mourning for the way their life is, for their failures, for their losses, for what should have been or could have been, for the unfairness of their lives, for how they are, for how they feel inside, for their past, for their wounded childhoods. People who consider themselves content but think *"I'll just add spirituality on as a cherry on top"* are never going to do deep inner work.

It is mourning that starts a person on the real inner journey.

"Blessed are those who mourn for they will be comforted."

Most people play dodgeball with their inner sadnesses. They are never truly comforted. Instead, they drown their mourning with drink and food and games and successes and pills and hobbies and judging others and blaming others and "faith".

Or they justify their mourning: *Oh, well, anyone would feel like this if they went through what I went through.* But the truth is that other people have been through worse and not been engulfed by meaninglessness.

Only inner work and inner healing can provide true comfort: only this can truly heal your inner sadnesses. Only inner work and inner healing can fill that void which you mourn.

This included Jesus. It included John the Baptist. Their paths started off with mourning.

What about you?

Are you currently mourning?

Are you discontented by your inner discontent?

In a confrontation with meaninglessness?

Depressed?

Consumed by the thought that there simply has to be more to life than this?

Take a deep breath.

This is the absolute precondition for starting on the path. It is the first step on the path of blessedness.

No mourning, no blessedness.

2. "Blessed are the meek..."

Vain people – people full of themselves – are never going to start on the path. They are never going to work on themselves. It does not matter how down and dispirited you are. If you are vainly convinced that you are superior to everyone else and already have all the answers, you won't start on the path of true inner evolution.

We have all known people who are miserable and mean-spirited yet still believe they are superior to others and have all the answers.

Right now, the single biggest barrier between you and the truth is thinking that you already have it. How meek are you in reading this book? Are you humble enough to be prepared to learn from it? Or are you reading it from a space of vanity? *I know more than this guy. I have faith. My spiritual faith insulates me from anything this crazy guy has to say... I KNOW...*

Or are you an atheist who is absolutely certain that they have the absolute truth, unlike those poor benighted primitives who believe in spirituality?

Such an absence of meekness will absolutely stall you from advancing in the path.

To take the second step on the path of blessedness, you have to be prepared to be a student and not puffed up by what you think you already know. You have to meekly admit that another person may have greater experience and knowledge than you do. This is one of the biggest benefits of mourning: it can force you to abandon the idea that you know it all, that you have all the answers. It can crumble the egoic props you've placed around yourself and expose you to greater truths.

Vanity is how the vast run of people plaster over their inner, gaping voids. They run a looping tape in their heads which repeats the mantra "*Mine is better than yours... Mine is better than yours... Mine is better than yours...*"*My knowledge, my integrity, my honesty, my faith, my career, my skills, my experience, my religion, my judgment, my cynicism, my beliefs, my university degrees, my bank balance, my hardships, my suffering, my excuses, my justifications, my certainty, my status, my fitness, my life partner, my family... something about me or my life* **is better than yours**.

Only mourning can prick the bubble of such vanity: making people meeker, humbler, and so open them up to new possibilities. Only mourning for what is missing in your life and inside you can snap the endless inner egoic defensive loop of "*Mine is better than yours*" and so open inner ears to the deeper voice that this egoic loop is covering up – the deep inner voice which whispers: "*There has to be more to life than this.*"

No mourning, no humility.

No humility, no blessedness.

"Blessed are the meek, for they will inherit the earth."

Note very carefully: "*inherit*".

Jesus does not say, "Blessed are the meek, for they will take possession of the earth"; nor does he say, "Blessed are the meek, for they shall conquer the earth". Rather, you *inherit it from someone else*. It is a gift from another person: something bequeathed to you from the life journey of another.

One of the greatest gifts of humility is that it enables you to inherit the knowledge and insights of other people. No humility, no capacity to learn from others. Jesus was able to learn from John the Baptist because he came to him as a humble student and so was able to inherit the wisdom and experience of John.

At this second stage of blessedness, what you inherit is not the kingdom of heaven; it is "the earth". Modern city folk generally have only a distant relationship with the earth. They do not understand its power. They think of it as something that dirties their shoes. To the ancients, earth was the ultimate source of life. Adam was said to be made out of the dust of the earth (Genesis 2:7). The earth produced plants – these plants fed the sons of Adam and their livestock. The earth was what they used to make their mud-brick homes. The earth was the source of all valuable metals. The earth housed them, supported them, fed them, enriched them. To inherit the earth is to inherit from another the soil on which you are empowered to grow and build a richly meaningful life.

> In the beginning, God created the heavens and the earth.
> - Genesis 1:1.

By being meek, one can inherit the earthly knowledge of others... but not, yet, the heavens.

3. "Blessed are those who hunger and thirst for rightness..."

The combination of mourning and meekness can be transmuted into something greater than the sum of the parts: an absolute burning hunger for rightness – to be right with yourself, to be right in yourself, to be right with life, to be right with your soul, your spirit. Only a deep and burning inner hunger can start you on the path and keep you on the path of inner transformation.

> "No one who puts his hand to the plow and looks back is fit for the kingdom of God."
> - Luke 9:62

This gaping hunger cannot be filled by money or toys or success or the esteem of others. It can only be filled through inner growth. Only this can fill you with a sense of real and permanent meaning.

The emptiness and void you mourn – the gaping maw where there should be meaningfulness – can only be filled by inner growth... ultimately by spiritual growth –spiritual growth that can culminate in being filled by the Holy Spirit.

No mourning, no humility.

No mourning and humility, no hunger for rightness.

No hunger for rightness, no blessedness.

"Blessed are those who hunger and thirst for righteousness for they will be filled." "Righteousness" has been the traditional "translation" for the original Greek word "dikaios". This Greek word could also be translated as: justice, straightness, equity, uprightness, trueness.[12]

The Greek word is sufficiently elusive that, in the 16th Century, the Bible translator William Tyndale felt the need to invent a new word to try to capture its flavor. That invented word was "righteousness". It was based on an older term "rihtwis" – "right wise" or "right ways". This invented word has gone on to influence a lot of Christian preaching.

The concept is even more elusive than even this suggests because Jesus did not speak Greek to his disciples. The closest Hebrew word is "tzadik," which could be translated as "one who is as he ought to be". The implication of "tzadik" is more internal and is more about being inwardly right with God. The Greek word "dikaios" came to be associated with "tzadik" even though that Greek word has more of a flavor of external relationships with

---

[12] See www.biblehub.com/greek/1342.htm for a discussion of "dikaios'.

others.[13] Despite these differences, the invented word "righteous" was used to "translate" both the Hebrew "tzadik" (in the Old Testament) and the Greek "dikaios" (in the New Testament).

It is even more complicated than this because Jesus would almost certainly not have spoken Hebrew to his disciples; he would have spoken Aramaic.

Given all this, I suggest that a far more suitable modern rendering is:

"Blessed are those who hunger and thirst for inner rightness for they will be filled."

The concepts "hunger", "thirst" and being "filled" are all terms about inner states so it is only logical to conclude that what Jesus had in mind was inner rightness – being right on the inside.

At any stage, a person can be stalled on the path to being filled by the Holy Spirit. One stage does not automatically lead to the next. You can mourn but this does not necessarily translate into meekness. You may still be trapped in vanity. *I may be miserable and empty inside but I'm still better than everyone else.*

You can mourn and be humbled but this does not automatically translate into a desperate hunger and thirst to be right on the inside. *Oh, yes, I'm miserable and, much to my surprise, I don't have all the answers in life after all... but it's other people who need to change, not me. The government needs to change. My wife needs to change. My kids need to change. My boss needs to change... NOT ME!*

---

[13] This association of dikaios with tzadik dates back to the Septuagint, the translation of Hebrew Scriptures into Greek that started in the 3rd Century B.C. There is a useful discussion of the translation problems surrounding "righteousness' in the Holman Bible Dictionary.

And, of course, some people never even mourn for the lack of meaning in their lives. Perhaps, through wealth or good fortune, they have never been thrown back on themselves.

> "It is easier for a camel to go through the eye of a needle than for a rich person to enter the kingdom of God."
> - Mark 10:25

But some people do get to the third stage along the path: they develop a burning hunger and thirst to be right on the inside. This way is not easy. It is not the way of averaged normality.

> "Enter by the narrow gate. For the gate is wide and the way is easy that leads to destruction, and those who enter by it are many. For the gate is narrow and the way is hard that leads to life, and those who find it are few."
> - Matthew 7:13-14

It is generally the people who have had fraught journeys through life who develop the hunger to be right on the inside, and turn away from the external world of fragile meaningfulness and turn towards the inner world where permanent meaningfulness can be forged. If you can convince yourself that you are content, you won't seek out and stick to deep inner work.

You have to have a lot of fuel to stay on the journey of deep inner transformation. A lot of fuel.

> "If anyone comes to me and does not hate his own father and mother and wife and children and brothers and sisters, yes, and even his own life, he cannot be my disciple."
> - Luke 14:26

Perhaps hardest of all: you have to be hungry and thirsty enough to be an individual and go your own way. Your friends can turn away from you. Your own family can oppose you. We have seen that Jesus's own family was ready to stage an intervention, thinking he'd entirely lost the plot.

When I started on deep personal growth work, my older brother later told me that he'd thought to himself, "*Oh, he's younger than me. He's naive. He'll learn.*" Later he came to embrace inner work himself. It became one of the greatest gifts of his fraught life – a life of coping with disability and epilepsy and a monstrous father.

> "Do you think that I have come to give peace on earth? No, I tell you, but rather division. For from now on in one house there will be five divided, three against two and two against three. They will be divided, father against son and son against father, mother against daughter and daughter against mother, mother-in-law against her daughter-in-law and daughter-in-law against mother-in-law."
>
> - Luke 12:51-53.

And I would say the same thing about this book. It's going to divide people. It's going to upset people. It's going to deeply challenge people. It's going to stir things up. It is going to infuriate some people – not because such people think it is wrong but because, deep down, they are afraid that it is right.

But for those who deeply hunger and thirst for inner rightness, this proper understanding of the path of the Beatitudes is more than just nourishment – it is manna from heaven.

There is another understanding that I have received from contemplating the path of the Beatitudes: there is a significant sense in which there are two subspecies of humans on the planet.

There are those who tread the trodden path; and then there is a second, different sub-species who have reached the third stage of the path of the Beatitudes: they have developed a burning thirst and an aching hunger to be right on the inside. They have committed to an inner path to find inner meaning. These two different sub-species can have significant difficulties communicating with each other. It is almost as if they live in different but overlapping universes. One sub-species looks towards an external universe and seeks meaning there – whether this be in external worldly success or in an external heaven. And then there is the sub-species who looks more towards an inner universe and seeks the path to genuine meaningfulness on the inside. The first sub-species regards the inner seekers as naïve, gullible, even self-centered. And, oddly enough, the sub-species of inner seekers often regard the first sub-species in pretty much the same way: naïve, gullible, even self-centered.

We may just have to accept that this communication gap between these two sub-species is not fully bridgeable and that, until a person reaches this third stage of having a deep hunger and thirst for inner rightness, they cannot be expected to fully comprehend talk of an inner path. At best, such talk is a map waiting for them should they and life ever take them to the third stage on the path of blessedness and they start to burn with a hunger and thirst to be right on the inside.

4. "Blessed are the merciful…"

The fourth step is to be merciful.

Mercy contains three components:

1. Forgiveness of others
2. Compassion for the suffering of others.

3. Purity of intent in action and in speech – never is one's primary intent to hurt others.

Cruelty and selfishness will assuredly block the path of spiritual growth.

This is where so many present-day self-appointed personal growth gurus have got it so badly wrong. They think that personal growth is about making people more confident, more "powerful", more motivated, more successful: to super-charge egos. Instead, the actual inner path must focus on developing a more merciful attitude toward others: forgiveness, compassion, purity of intent.

We have to forgive others – even those others who have done the gravest of wrongs to us. This doesn't mean that we have to keep them in our lives but we have to find a way to forgive them.

I have seen people lose their way in personal growth work because they thought that inner work would give them what "they" (their egos) wanted. They did the techniques of personal growth but they did not grow. Sometimes they regressed and became more selfish. And so it was that their path turned back on itself and stagnated. And they did not receive the mercy of true spiritual growth and meaningfulness. I remember one young woman in particular who did a huge number of inner work sessions but she would not let go of her desire for revenge against her parents. She ended up having a nervous breakdown.

Without compassion for others – without forgiveness of others – without purity of intent towards others – the path of blessedness cannot move forward.

This pinpoints the single biggest mistake of the "New Age" or "Personal Growth" movement: teachers failed to emphasize the importance of compassion and forgiveness and purity of intent. Instead, personal growth was portrayed as something that you did in order to manifest success in the external world: by doing inner work, you would magically manifest an outwardly golden life (money, success, worldly goods, fame, magical relationships, etc) and *then* you could be happy. If what you did or said made other people unhappy well that was just "their stuff" and their responsibility. Many people took this as a carte blanche to think and act out of self-centeredness.

A friend of mine did a number of Anthony Robbins courses. She told me about the aftermath of a fire-walking challenge when a group of them (including her) made fun of a guy who had got the soles of his feet burnt.

So much for human compassion.

And so it is that the inner path of many seekers had been blocked and looped around and did not move forward.

What is an absolute psychological precondition for having true compassion for others?

A significant degree of humility.

How can you have true compassion for others if you believe that you are superior to those inferior beings? You won't feel genuine compassion towards them. At best, you'll feel pity for those poor benighted people who are inferior to you.

Think about the vain people you've known – or seen on TV. These are the people who think they know it all, who think they are better than others – intellectually, genetically, socially, culturally, nationally, religiously superior to other people. *Mine is better than yours.* Do you see in these people any real and genuine compassion for humanity?

These are the Adolf Hitlers. The religious terrorists and fanatics. The worst of the self-satisfiedly arrogant atheists. The Stalins. The know-it-all talking heads on TV.

By contrast, when we see the iconically compassionate – Gandhi, Irena Sendler, Jesus – we see humility made flesh.

No mourning, no humility.

No humility, no mercy for others.

No mercy for others, no blessedness.

"Blessed are the merciful for they will receive mercy."

We are all imperfect. We have all committed imperfect acts. We will always be imperfect – no matter how much inner work we do. Jesus said that he was not perfect, not good (Mark 10:18). But, by cultivating mercy towards others, we can experience mercy for our past and present failings... and hopefully receive the ultimate mercy of baptism by the Holy Spirit.

In the case of Jesus, surely his strongest suit was compassion for others – even to the point of allowing himself to be cast into the agony of crucifixion because he believed that, in so doing, he would become a "ransom for many" (Mark 10:45).

It is not enough to do deeds that look good from the outside. You have to have true purity of intent towards others. *As you do, so you tend to become.* Pure intentions tend to make you more pure on the inside. Evil intentions cloud your soul. To advance along the path of blessedness, you have to set high standards for yourself. *Steal a million dollars, you're a thief. Steal five cents, you're a thief.*

> "One who is faithful in a very little is also faithful
> in much, and one who is dishonest in a very little
> is also dishonest in much."
> - Luke 16:10

But outer actions are not enough. You have to have purity of intent on the inside.

"You have heard that it was said, 'You shall not commit adultery.' But I say to you that everyone who looks at a woman with lustful intent has already committed adultery with her in his heart. If your right eye causes you to sin, tear it out and throw it away. For it is better that you lose one of your members than that your whole body be thrown into hell. And if your right hand causes you to sin, cut it off and throw it away. For it is better that you lose one of your members than that your whole body go into hell."

- Matthew 5:27-30

Why do you need purity of intent to have a chance at baptism by the Holy Spirit? Because the Holy Spirit is pure. If you are to merge with it, you have to become like it. You have no chance of doing this if you are constantly clouding your soul with vindictive actions and nasty intentions toward others.

...this light cannot shine or lighten in sinners that is why this birth cannot possibly occur in them. This birth cannot coexist with the darkness of sin, even though it takes place, not in the powers, but in the essence and ground of the soul.

- Meister Eckhart, *Complete Mystical Works of Meister Eckhart*, Sermon 2, p. 41.

Lack of mercy – lack of forgiveness, lack of compassion, impurity of intent – will surely stain your soul and block the path of blessedness.

The quality of mercy... is twice blest: It blesseth him that gives and him that takes.

- Shakespeare, *The Merchant of Venice*, IV, ii.

5. "Blessed are the pure in heart...."

The fifth step moves us into the great spiritual inner work.

Mercy, the fourth step, is the start of building inner purity. But you also have to do direct transformative work on purifying your innermost self: your heart, your energies, your soul.

This is the great alchemical spiritual work: detraumatize your energies back to what they were at the very beginning. A sign that your soul is being purified is that you will experience spiritual visions. This is the fifth step of blessedness.

Many people conflate mysticism with the having of visions. They think that this is what the mystic path is all about – even thinking that receiving visions is the goal of the inner path.

It isn't.

Genuine visions are a by-product of inner purification – a by-product of becoming "pure in heart".

"Blessed are the pure in heart, for they will see God."

Nowadays, genuine spiritual visions are likely to involve at least some visions of Jesus.[14]

Falling in love with spiritual visions can be a big trap along the inner path.

> Even if individuals are so shrewd, humble, and strong that the devil is unable to deceive them by these visions or make them (as he usually does) fall into any presumption, the visions will be an obstacle to their advancement if they fail to practice this denial, since visions are an

---

[14] The reason for this is explained in *The Crucifixion Code*.

> impediment to spiritual nakedness, poverty of spirit, and emptiness in faith; these are the requisites for union with God.
>
> - St John of the Cross, *The Ascent of Carmel* 24:9, p. 244.

I am reminded of one young woman I knew who did a lot of inner work sessions but fell in love with her experiences of an apparent past life as a high priestess. She looped around and around and round in these experiences seemingly endlessly, session after session.

Visions may be all very impressive and impress you and impress others but they are only a stage along the path. Further purification of the soul is needed to go beyond the level of visions.

(Purification of the soul will be discussed in more detail in Part IV.)

6. "Blessed are the peace-makers..."

A stage beyond visions is the direct experience of the purified energy in your soul.

When you totally purify a traumatized energy in your soul, it reverts into its original, untraumatized, pure form. You will experience this as pure Love, pure Peace, pure Beingness, pure Consciousness... This is the Peace that passes all understanding. Mystics sometimes refer to such experiences as experiences of "Essence" – you are back at the very essence of your soul before it was traumatized.[15]

This is the sixth stage of blessedness – the stage beyond visions – the stage where you are making Peace in your soul.

---

[15] See, for instance, A.H. Almaas, *Essence*.

With more inner work, more and more of your soul becomes purified. You make more and more "Peace" within your soul. Your soul can now be likened unto a child – like a baby before it was traumatized by its journey through life. Jesus used the analogy of infants and children to represent the purified soul.

> "Truly, I say to you, whoever does not receive the kingdom of God like a child shall not enter it."
> - Mark 10:15

To get to this level, you have to detraumatize your soul, purify it, transform traumatized energies back into the original Essence energies of Peace, Love, Beingness.

"Blessed are the peace-makers, for they will be called children of God."

It does not get much higher than to be deemed "a child of God". This signifies that the energies of your soul are back where they were before your soul was traumatized by its journey through time.[16] It means your soul is now ready to enter the kingdom of heaven – i.e., to be baptized by the Holy Spirit.

Notice that you *make* peace. It is an active process. It requires inner work.

There is only one stage higher than being "a child of God': the realization of the kingdom of heaven... baptism by the Holy Spirit.

The Seven Stages of Blessedness

The "making of peace" makes possible a seventh step: to be baptized by the Holy Spirit. This step is out of your control. Deep inner transformative work will get you to the door where you can

---

[16] Discussed in more detail in *The Crucifixion Code*.

knock and keep knocking but you have to wait for it to be opened to you (Matt 7:7-11). Should the door open, you will be baptized by the Holy Spirit: your soul and the Holy Spirit will fuse, and so your transformed soul will become part of the kingdom of heaven. Your soul will become truly "blessed" – filled with the divine.

"Blessed are the poor in spirit, for theirs is the kingdom of heaven."

This then is the great journey of "the poor in spirit". Poverty of spirit makes it possible to break out of the loop of normality and go on the journey of the Seven Steps:

1. **Mourning**
2. **Meekness**
3. **Hunger for inner rightness**
4. **Mercy**
5. **Purification occasioning visions**
6. **Further purification occasioning the making of Peace in your soul.**
7. **Baptism by the Holy Spirit (realizing the kingdom of heaven)**

The Beatitudes is easily – far and away – the best summary I have ever found of the path of genuine inner transformation.

Indeed, it is the only summary I have ever found.

Its succinctness, its insights, its incisiveness stagger me.

The Beatitudes: A personal reflection

When I started writing The Jesus Code, I had no idea that the Beatitudes constituted a crystalline outline of the path of inner transformation. But I found myself quoting four of the Beatitudes when I was trying to elucidate the mystic path so I thought: "*Give me a closer look at the Beatitudes.*"

And I was amazed... stunned.

This was the great gift I received out of writing *The Jesus Code*: to realize that the Beatitudes constitute a clear step-by-step outline of the path of inner transformation. The more I contemplate The Beatitudes, the more in awe I am.

I can quote mystics on the latter stages of inner growth: visions, purification, experiences of peace, the need for compassion for others. But the Beatitudes outline the exact psychological/emotional steps that even get you to the inner path in the first place: mourning... being humbled by that mourning... leading to a hunger and thirst to be right on the inside.

Even the most atheistic of psychologists and psychiatrists will surely recognize these first three steps as what gets a client to a therapist's door. The person aches for more meaning in their life. (They mourn.) This breaks through their egoic props and convinces them that they might not know it all. (They have been meekened.) The combination of these makes the person hunger to be right on the inside: *something inside me has to change – the external world is not going to do it for me.* And this gets them to the door of the therapist's office.

And, once they come through that door, what are psychologists trying to support their clients in doing?

The path of the Beatitudes suggests that psychologists and psychiatrists should be focusing on three things:

1. Building emotional maturity in their clients through the practice of forgiveness, compassion and purity of intent (*Blessed are the merciful*)

2. Supporting traumatized people in becoming less traumatized. (*Blessed are the pure in heart* - what we would now call "detraumatization" ancient mystics commonly referred to as "purification".)

3. Helping the distressed to become people less distressed, more peaceful (*Blessed are the peace-makers*)

Indeed, this is what a lot of psychologists do try to do.

The Beatitudes: the huge journey of psychological and spiritual transformation laid out in seven short sentences. There is no doubt in my mind that it is this knowledge – hiding in plain sight for two thousand years – which is most needed by anyone seeking genuine meaning in life. It was the lack of this knowledge which turned so much of the "New Age" or "Personal Growth" movement into a venal cult aimed at producing "successful" people who are into "positive thinking" and external "abundance".

It was this level of clarity which was lacking even in the most cherished of my spiritual teachers.

It was this knowledge that was lacking in me at key times of decision in my life.

And I never saw it coming when I started writing *The Jesus Code*.

This decoding of the Beatitudes is the clinching proof that Jesus was a mystic preaching the inner path of the transformation of the soul. It makes sense of what previously did not make sense: The Beatitudes. Beyond even that, the Beatitudes clarify in unbelievable succinctness the exact steps of the path of inner transformation.

Have you ever wondered what mysticism is?

It is a path.

And that path is laid out step-by-step in the Beatitudes.

Seven steps.

Seven sentences.

Staggering.

Did Matthew understand the Beatitudes?

So here is a fascinating question: Did "Matthew" – the flesh-and-blood person who wrote down that Gospel – actually understand that the Beatitudes spelt out the path of inner spiritual transformation? Or was he just mindlessly copying down something with no understanding of what it meant?

I believe he absolutely understood.

Let us contrast the Gospel of Matthew with the Gospel of Luke. The author of the Gospel of Luke was plainly oblivious about the import of the Beatitudes. Instead of having the Beatitudes set on a mountain and said in private to his disciples, Luke has Jesus come down off the mountain and talk to a great crowd:

> In these days he went out to the mountain to pray, and all night he continued in prayer to God... And he came down with them and stood on a level place, with a great crowd of his disciples and a great multitude of people from all Judea and Jerusalem and the seacoast of Tyre and Sidon...
> - Luke 6:12,17

This is symptomatic of Luke's passion for inclusiveness. Whereas Matthew was writing with only a Jewish audience in mind, Luke was writing with Gentiles and Jews in mind so he did not want to portray a teaching as being reserved for a few Jews. Nevertheless, Luke concedes that Jesus was actually addressing his disciples: "And he lifted up his eyes on his disciples, and said..." (Luke 6.20)

Luke is so clueless about the import of the Beatitudes that he leaves most of them out and castrates the ones he leaves in. In the case of the first beatitude, he literally rips the spirit out of it:

> "Blessed are you who are poor, for yours is the kingdom of God.
> Blessed are you who are hungry now, for you shall be satisfied.
> Blessed are you who weep now, for you shall laugh.
> Blessed are you when people hate you and when they exclude you and revile you and spurn your name as evil, on account of the Son of Man! Rejoice in that day, and leap for joy, for behold, your reward is great in heaven; for so their fathers did to the prophets."
> — Luke 6:20-23

Luke omitted and altered Beatitudes because he could not make sense of them in earthly terms... because they make no sense in earthly terms. They only make sense in terms of the inner path of transformation.

By contrast, Matthew understands the Beatitudes to be so pivotal that he has this teaching come forth on a mountain – just like the Ten Commandments. Matthew makes the Beatitudes into the very first speech that Jesus gives – the very first thing that he teaches his disciples. The Gospel of Matthew is structured around this enshrinement of the Beatitudes. Indeed, the entire Gospel of Matthew can be regarded as an argument that the Beatitudes constitute a higher level of spiritual knowledge than the Ten Commandments and the Law of Moses.

Straight after the Beatitudes, Jesus says that following these steps will make the disciples into the "salt of the earth" and "the light of the world" (Matt 5:13-14). Jesus then goes on to say that to realize the kingdom of heaven, you have to exceed the old level of rightness or "righteousness". You cannot just obey the Law of Moses:

> For I tell you, unless your righteousness exceeds
> that of the scribes and Pharisees, you will never
> enter the kingdom of heaven. (Matt 5:20)

Then Jesus gives examples of how you have to go beyond the Ten Commandments and the old Law:

- Not only shalt thou not commit murder but do not insult; and fight against inner anger (Matt 5:21-24)
- Not only shalt thou not commit adultery, but don't even lust inappropriately (Matt 5:27-30)
- No long can you take an eye for an eye, but you have to turn the other cheek (Matt 5:38-41)

Matthew recognized that the Beatitudes meant that the old covenant of Moses had been superseded. Replacing it was a modified (or "fulfilled') covenant in which the realization of "the kingdom of heaven" was pivotal. (See Matt 5:17.)

This explains just why Matthew was so concerned to portray Jesus as the second Moses and have him come out of Egypt just as Moses did (Matt 2:13-14, 19-20).[17] Jesus was the new, improved, second Moses bringing a revised covenant from a mountain which would supersede even the Ten Commandments and the Law of Moses.

Also telling is that the Gospel of Matthew is the only Gospel that, instead of just using the phrase "kingdom of God" (*Basileia tou Theo*), mainly uses the phrase "kingdom of heaven" (*Basileia tōn*

---

[17] More on Matthew's portrayal of Jesus as the Second Moses in Appendix Two.

Ouranōs). Why did Matthew make this change? I think it was because he wanted to signify that this "kingdom" was very much a spiritual kingdom, not earthly in any way. It was of "heaven" – where God and spirit dwell. Absolutely not of this physical world. Possibly Matthew was trying to guard against the exact mistake that academics (and many others) have made – thinking that "the kingdom of God" was a reference to an earthly kingdom. Furthermore, as we shall soon see, much of the rest of the Sermon on the Mount in the Gospel of Matthew is an amalgam of Jesus's thoughts on just how dedicated to the inner path you have to be to realize "the kingdom of heaven".

Unlike the author of the Gospel of Luke, Matthew heard and understood.

Beatitude #8: The Disclaimer

Having outlined the seven steps in the transformation of the soul, Jesus warns his disciples that this inner work won't necessarily give them an easy life. They may be challenged both before and after they realize the kingdom of God. They have separated themselves from averaged normality. They cannot expect an easy outer life just because they have a more evolved inner life.

"Blessed are those who are persecuted for the sake of rightness, for theirs is the kingdom of heaven."

This is a remarkable caveat.

Adhering to the ways of the Old Covenant of Moses was supposed to guarantee a good life: obey the Ten Commandments and the Law, and then God will look after the nation of Israel – and presumably you. But now Jesus says no: obey the higher covenant of the Beatitudes and you may still be persecuted but the kingdom of heaven will be yours – you will be "blessed" – you will be baptized by the Holy Spirit. You will have lasting and permanent inner meaning.

This is the Law of Sacrifice in action: if you want a major change, you have to be prepared to make a sacrifice. If you want an answer, be prepared for a challenging question. If you want to go on the path less traveled, expect opposition from those shielding themselves in the cloak of averaged normality.

This is so far the opposite of what most "New Age" teachers spruik. They delude their students into thinking that inner spiritual growth will result in an easy outer life. I once had a ridiculous conversation with a man who had just completed a New Age money-consciousness course, during which he confidently informed me that someone's wealth is a measure of how spiritually evolved they are.

Good grief.

So rich drug dealers and the insider traders on Wall Street are spiritually evolved whereas Jesus and Buddha are down the bottom of the spiritual ladder because they were poor? How can there be people out there teaching crap like that?

But, in a way, this ludicrous belief harks back to the old pagan beliefs: do the right thing by God/gods and you will be rewarded in this life.

But no such guarantee exists under the inner path of the Beatitudes. Instead, the inner path results in inner meaning, permanent meaning, treasure in heaven, a transformed soul that endures beyond physical death. It does not mean the magical manifestation of wealth and great relationships and a comfy life. Indeed, the easy life is what can stymie you from doing inner work.

Remember the first step on the path of blessedness: you have to mourn... no mourning, no blessedness.

Jesus tells the disciples that, should they realize the kingdom of God, they have an obligation to become a light to others who are still in darkness: "You are the light of the world. A city set on a hill cannot be hidden. Nor do people light a lamp and put it under a basket, but on a stand, and it gives light to all in the house. In the same way, let your light shine before others..." (Matt 5:14-16).

After the Beatitudes, the Gospel of Matthew records the rest of the "Sermon on the Mount". A significant proportion of this consists in explaining the very high standards you have to set yourself in order to achieve true purity of intention towards others and so start to become "pure in heart". Jesus emphasizes not just doing the right thing on the outside but creating purity on the inside:

- Love not just those who love you but love also your enemies (Matt 5:43-47)
- Give freely to others from your heart and not to win admiration from others (Matt 6:2-4).

Jesus also emphasizes how incredibly focused you have to be to get to baptism by the Holy Spirit and so realize the kingdom of God inside:

- Pray for the kingdom of heaven to come within you (Matt 6:10)
- Focus not on earthly treasures but on the treasures you can build up in your soul (Matt 6:19-21)
- Prioritize inner spiritual evolution above all else because no-one can serve two masters (Matt 6:24)
- Prioritize it even above concerns about food, drink, clothing (Matt 6:25-34)

Hear but not understand

The Beatitudes clarify one reason why Jesus spoke in parables to the general populace and could not bring himself to attempt to explain the kingdom of God to the masses: you have to be at some stage along the path of blessedness to truly hear.

A spiritual teacher – a Jesus or a John the Baptist – cannot take you along the first three steps of the path of blessedness. You have to tread those by yourself. You have to mourn. You have to be humbled. You have to hunger and thirst to be right on the inside. Only then are you ready for the teacher. Only then are you ready to truly hear. Only then are you ready to commit.

If you are carefree and happy, you will simply dismiss anything that might blow a gust of wind toward your house of cards. (You don't think your life is a house of cards? Almost everyone is one or two sentences away from the void. I *don't love you... I never loved you... I'm having sex with someone else... I've fallen in love with someone else... You have cancer... You're fired... You're bankrupt... You're going to lose everything... Your children have all been killed in a car accident... You'll never walk again... You've got two months left to live...* The truth is that earthly life is fragile.)

As it was in Jesus's time, so it is now.

Right now, there is no point in talking about the inner journey to those who have never mourned, who have no humility, who are devoid of the hunger and of thirst to be right on the inside. They are living in a different universe. Their inner world is swamped by inner voices assuring them how wonderful they are, how right they are, how clever they are, how great their life is, how much they know, or – perhaps – how much they have out-suffered other people. *Mine is better than yours.* Such people are – at least temporarily –

plastering over the relentless deep inner voice whispering, *"There has to be more to life than this."*

Inevitably, this includes many readers of this book. Unless you have at some stage mourned for the lack of meaning in your life, this book will just become fodder for those inner parts of you which are convinced that they are clever and knowledgeable. They will dismiss this book. They will believe they can disprove it. Should they fail in this, they will, unabashed, turn to attacking the character or qualifications of the author. Without realizing what they are doing, they will cast themselves into the role of the high priests saying: "By what authority are you writing these things?"[18]

Yet... someday... mourning may force meekness and a hunger to be right on the inside... then the Beatitudes can speak to you... then there is a chance to not just hear but understand... and to understand not just the Beatitudes but also...

The Lord's Prayer

Surely the best-known words in the New Testament are those of the so-called "Lord's Prayer". There is probably no other passage of such a length which has been memorized by such a huge proportion of the human race:

> Our Father which art in heaven, Hallowed be thy name.
> Thy kingdom come. Thy will be done on earth, as it is in heaven.
> Give us this day our daily bread.
> And forgive us our trespasses, as we forgive those who trespass against us.

---

[18] ...the chief priests and the scribes and the elders came to him [Jesus], and they said to him, "By what authority are you doing these things, or who gave you this authority to do them?" (Mark 11:27-28).

> And lead us not into temptation, but deliver us
> from evil
> > - Matthew 6:9-13 (Book of Common
> > Prayer)

If you've ever been to church or seen a church service, you will have heard people pray this out loud as a group. Ironically, this is exactly the opposite of what Jesus said to do:

> "And when you pray, you must not be like the hypocrites. For they love to stand and pray in the synagogues and at the street corners, that they may be seen by others. Truly, I say to you, they have received their reward. But when you pray, go into your room and shut the door and pray to your Father who is in secret. And your Father who sees in secret will reward you."
> > - Matthew 6:5-6

So this prayer is supposed to be a *private* prayer – just between the supplicant and the Father. Moreover, it is also the *only* prayer needed:

> "And when you pray, do not heap up empty phrases as the Gentiles do, for they think that they will be heard for their many words. Do not be like them, for your Father knows what you need before you ask him. Pray then like this: Our Father in heaven..."
> > - Matthew 6:7-9

The Gospel of Luke makes it plain that the Lord's Prayer was given by Jesus only to his disciples – disciples who were trying to realize the kingdom of God:

> Now Jesus was praying in a certain place, and when he finished, one of his disciples said to him,

"Lord, teach us to pray, as John taught his disciples." And he said to them, "When you pray, say:
"Father, hallowed be your name.
Your kingdom come.
Give us each day our daily bread,
and forgive us our sins,
for we ourselves forgive everyone who is indebted to us.
And lead us not into temptation."

- Luke 11:1-4

Remarkably, this passage makes it clear that the Lord's Prayer originated not with Jesus but instead came from John the Baptist and that he taught it only to disciples. As Jesus knows the prayer, the inescapable conclusion is that Jesus was a disciple of the Baptist and, in turn, is now passing John's prayer on to his own disciples. Arguably, it should never have been known as "The Lord's Prayer" but as "John the Baptist's Prayer". Even more appropriate would be to refer to it as "The Disciple's Prayer". It is a prayer specifically for disciples: for those dedicated to the path of the Beatitudes, the path of the transformation of the soul.

Let us look in detail at this private spiritual petition:

"Our Father"

Notice the appellation is "*Our* Father". God is everyone's father. Not just Jesus's. We are each and all the offspring of God.[19]

"which art in heaven"

God is not everywhere; he is not omnipresent. He is distant. He is in the kingdom of heaven. He dwells in and on the Holy Spirit ("heaven").

---

[19] For an explanation of this, see *The Crucifixion Code*.

"Thy kingdom come."

Straight after calling God comes the first, most urgent petition: a plea for the kingdom of heaven to come within the soul of the supplicant – i.e., to undergo baptism by the Holy Spirit.

Note once again that this prayer is a *private* plea. If the coming of "the kingdom of God" was to be a public post-apocalyptic kingdom on earth then it would have made more sense if the disciples prayed for this as a group. Moreover, if "the kingdom of God" was a reference to the establishment of a physical kingdom of God on earth then why oh why would Jesus teach his disciples to pray for something that was inevitably going to happen because God was going to make it happen?

"Thy will be done on earth, as it is in heaven."

Once the kingdom of heaven has come within the soul, the supplicant can become a vehicle for divine will. Notice that God's will is not currently being done on Earth otherwise there would be no need to pray for it.

"Give us this day our daily bread."

So now we come to the consideration of the single most fascinating word in the entire New Testament: επιούσιος (*epiousios*). "Give us this day our *epiousios* bread." This is the only appearance of this Greek word which has ever been found not just in the Bible but anywhere. It has traditionally been unforgivably mistranslated as "daily".

This word is so singularly unique that epiousios must surely be a coinage by a translator (a Greek-speaking bilingual disciple of Jesus perhaps?) trying to capture the flavor of the original Aramaic. It is a composite of two Greek words:

- *Epi* meaning "upon", "on" or "over" as in *epidermis* (the top layer of skin) and *epicenter* (the point on the earth's surface directly above the center of an earthquake);

- *Ousia* meaning "substance" or "essence" or "being".

When St Jerome did his landmark translation of the New Testament into Latin (the Vulgate), he felt the need to coin a new Latin word to capture the flavor of the coined Greek word. So he invented the word *supersubstantialem* ("supersubstantial"). "Give us this day our supersubstantial (above-substance) bread".

One thing we can be certain of is that it is not a reference to physical or "daily" bread.

In more modern vernacular, we would render "epiousios" as "higher being" (epi-ousia): "Give us this day our higher-being bread".

If ever there was a one-word proof that Jesus was a mystic teaching the transformation of the soul and that this concept stretched the understanding, images and vocabulary of everyday conversation, it is surely this word and its reference to higher being.

In no way is this a petition to God to keep our stomachs full. Jesus explicitly said that spiritual concerns should outweigh concerns even about food:

> "Therefore do not be anxious, saying, 'What shall we eat?' or 'What shall we drink?' or 'What shall we wear?' For the Gentiles seek after all these things, and your heavenly Father knows that you need them all. But seek first the kingdom of God..."
>
> - Matthew 6:31-33

If you're not supposed to be anxious about food, why would Jesus be teaching his disciples to pray for it???

One possible interpretation is that this is a petition for spiritual sustenance rather than physical sustenance: an appeal for the inner strength to stay on the path. But there is another possibility: that this petition is another way of appealing for baptism by the Holy Spirit. Bread is one of Jesus's favored images for explaining the transformation of the soul:

> "The kingdom of heaven is like yeast that a woman took and mixed with three measures of flour until all of it was leavened."
> - Matthew 13:33 (ISV)

If this is what Jesus said in brief to the masses, he very probably expounded more on this in private to his disciples so that they understood that the appeal for "*epiousios* (higher-being) bread" is an appeal for the soul (the flour) to be merged with and raised up by the yeast of the Holy Spirit.

This would make this a petition for the transformation of the soul: to have the soul raised up higher by the Holy Spirit just as bread is raised up higher by yeast... And for this to happen on this very day: "Give us THIS day...'

"And forgive us our trespasses, as we forgive those who trespass against us."

This correlates with the Beatitude: "*Blessed are the merciful for they will receive mercy.*" Are you perfect? No? Do you want to be forgiven for being less than perfect? Then you have to forgive. If you don't have mercy and forgive others, you will never be baptized by the Holy Spirit.

"And lead us not into temptation"

This correlates with the Beatitude: "*Blessed are the pure in heart...*" You are never going to achieve purity of heart if you give in to the darker demons of your nature.

"But deliver us from evil"

Deliver us both from our inner evil and from outer evil.

Doubtless, there are many, many readers out who are now silently screaming: "No, no. No!!! This is too long a bow. This is stretching things too far. All that stuff about 'epiousios', it's just nonsense. You're trying to confuse something which has always been perfectly clear. There is simply no way that the Lord's Prayer is a plea for baptism by the Holy Spirit."

Oh really? So let's just look at what Jesus says to his disciples immediately after teaching them the prayer:

> And he said to them, "Which of you who has a friend will go to him at midnight and say to him, 'Friend, lend me three loaves, for a friend of mine has arrived on a journey, and I have nothing to set before him'; and he will answer from within, 'Do not bother me; the door is now shut, and my children are with me in bed. I cannot get up and give you anything'? I tell you, though he will not get up and give him anything because he is his friend, yet because of his impudence he will rise and give him whatever he needs. And I tell you, ask, and it will be given to you; seek, and you will find; knock, and it will be opened to you. For everyone who asks receives, and the one who seeks finds, and to the one who knocks it will be opened. What father among you, if his son asks for a fish, will instead of a fish give him a serpent;

> or if he asks for an egg, will give him a scorpion?
> If you then, who are evil, know how to give good
> gifts to your children, how much more will the
> heavenly Father give the Holy Spirit to those who
> ask him!"
>
> - Luke 11:5-13

So there you have it: the clarification of the purpose of the prayer straight from Jesus's lips. The prayer is an appeal to the heavenly Father to bestow the Holy Spirit upon the supplicant.

(Out of the billions of times this prayer has been repeated, how many supplicants do you suppose have actually been aware that what they are reciting is supposed to be an impassioned plea to be baptized by the Holy Spirit?)

Surely this disciple's prayer which calls for the kingdom to come ("your kingdom come") followed by Jesus's clarification that this prayer is a request that "the heavenly Father give the Holy Spirit" is clinching proof that the coming of the kingdom of God and baptism by the Holy Spirit are basically one and the same.

The Beatitudes is a step-by-step guide to make a disciple's soul ready for baptism by the Holy Spirit. "The Lord's Prayer" is a private plea to the heavenly Father to bestow upon the supplicant baptism by the Holy Spirit.

Q.E.D. Quod Erat Demonstrandum. That which was requiring to be proved is proven. For Jesus and John the Baptist, the "coming of the kingdom of God" and "baptism by the Holy Spirit" were one and the same.

But not all aspects of the mystic mystery have been solved. For in places Jesus does not refer to the *coming* of the kingdom of God[20]

---

[20] For further examples see Matthew 12:28; Luke 17:20.

but rather *entry* into the kingdom of God/heaven[21]. Why did he do this?

To understand this we are going to have to better understand baptism by the Holy Spirit.

---

[21] See Matthew 5:20, 7:21, 18-3, 19-23, 19-24, 21-31, 23-13; Mark 9-47,. 10:15, 10:23-25; Luke 18-17, 18-24, 18:25; John 3:5.

Part IV

Baptism by the Holy Spirit

"Truly, I say to you, whoever does not receive the
kingdom of God like a child shall not enter it."

- Mark 10:14-15

The Path of Blessedness

In this fourth part, we will be concentrating on the later stages of the Beatitudes' path of blessedness: the purification of the soul (steps five and six) and baptism by the Holy Spirit (step seven, the culmination).

Purification/detraumatization of the soul

Mystics across the ages have emphasized that the soul needs to be "purified".

The 1st Century Jewish historian, Josephus, writes more about John the Baptist than he does about Jesus and his portrayal of John emphasizes purification:

> For Herod had executed him, though he was a good man and had urged the Jews – if inclined to exercise virtue, to practice justice toward one another and piety toward God – to join in baptism. For baptizing was acceptable to him [i.e., God], not for pardon of whatever sins they may have committed, but in purifying the body, as though the soul had beforehand been cleansed in righteousness.
>
> - Josephus, *Antiquities of the Jews*[22]

In being purified, the energies of the soul are turned back into what they were at the very beginning... the VERY beginning ... before

---

[22] See Craig AA. Evans, "Josephus on John the Baptist and Other Jewish Prophets of Deliverance' in Amy-Jill Levine et al (ed.), *The Historical Jesus in Context*, p. 60.

the soul was even born. In modern terms, we would say that the soul has to be de-traumatized.

> The disciples said to Jesus, "Tell us how will our end come?"
> Jesus said, "Have you found the beginning, then, that you are looking for the end?
> You see, the end will be where the beginning is. Congratulations to the one who stands at the beginning: that one will know the end and will not taste death."
> – Gospel of Thomas 18

> The Lord says: "Blest is he who is before he comes into Being!" For he who is, both was and shall be...
> – Gospel of Philip, 61

Jesus instructs that the soul must become pure and unsullied: like as to a baby that has yet to be traumatized by life.

> Jesus saw infants being suckled. He said to his disciples, "These infants being suckled are like those who enter the kingdom."
> – Gospel of Thomas 22

The Biblical Gospels record this analogy as being about young children:

> "Let the children come to me; do not hinder them, for to such belongs the kingdom of God. Truly, I say to you, whoever does not receive the kingdom of God like a child shall not enter it."
> – Mark 10:14-15

Let us look at what other mystics said about the purification of the soul and the need to turn the soul back into what it was at the very beginning:

106

But those who are pure in heart, who practice
Meditation and conquer their senses
And passions, shall attain the immortal Self,
Source of all light and source of all life.
>   - Mundaka Upanishad I, 2.11, p.111.

...man should be not only righteous, but sanctified and purified in advance in soul and body by keeping the divine commandments, and so be transformed into a vehicle worthy to receive the all-powerful Spirit...
>   - St Gregory of Palamas, *The Triads*, III iii 5, pp. 103-4.

...it is that the Soul has become again what it was formerly, when it was blessed.
>   - Plotinus, *The Enneads*, VI, 7, 34, p.135.[23]

...the One, and Beauty, and Righteousness, and Virtue... these are the offspring of a Soul which is filled with God, and this is its beginning and end – its beginning because from this it had its origin, its end because the Good is there, and when it comes there it becomes what it was.
>   - Plotinus, *The Enneads* VI, 9, 9. p.139.

...why then do we not become wise? ...The most important factor is to break through and beyond all things and The Origin of All Things, and it is this process that weighs us down.
>   - Meister Eckhart, *Selected Writings*, p.170.

---

[23] Quotes from Plotinus are from the W.R. Inge translation, *The Philosophy of Plotinus* (New York: Longmans, Green & Co: 3rd Edition, 1929) Vol II, pp.134-43.

Baptism by the Holy Spirit

The soul will never become totally and utterly purified. That is impossible. That is something that Jesus himself abjured:

> As he was setting out on a journey, a man ran up and knelt before him and asked him, "Good Teacher, what must I do to inherit eternal life?" Jesus said to him, "Why do you call me good? No-one is good..."
>
> - Mark 10:17-18

No-one and no soul can become totally pure. But the soul can become sufficiently purified that it is close to the vibrations of the Holy-Spirit/The-One/Brahman running through it. When it is sufficiently purified – sufficiently de-traumatized – a dramatic once-only-ever event can happen.

The soul is baptized by the Holy Spirit.

The soul and the underlying Spirit become one.

Fused.

Joined.

Forever.

And in so doing, the soul enters into the kingdom of God.

> They said to him, "Shall we then, as children, enter the kingdom?"
> Jesus said to them, "When you make the two one... then will you enter [the kingdom]."
>
> - Gospel of Thomas 22

The two become one. The yeast (the Holy Spirit) underlying the flour (the soul) leavens the bread, raising it up. The leavened bread is the "Son" of the flour and the yeast. When the Holy Spirit and soul fuse, they produce something that is greater than either separately: a "Son". This can only be done if the soul is made like the Holy Spirit:

"No one puts new wine into old wineskins; otherwise the wine will burst the skins, and the wine is lost and the skins as well; but one puts new wine into fresh wineskins."

> \- Mark 2:22

Let us look at how other mystics have described this process of purification and fusion:

...those judged worthy of this grace know that it is not a fantasy produced by the imagination, and that it does not originate with us, nor appear only to disappear; but rather, it is a permanent energy produced by grace, united to the soul and rooted in it...

> \- St Gregory of Palamas, *The Triads*, II ii 9, p. 50.

"I have realized the Self," declares the sage,
"Who is present in all beings.
I am united with the Lord of Love;
I am united with the Lord of Love."

> \- Amritabindu Upanishad 22, p.244.

As a lump of salt thrown in water dissolves and cannot be taken out again, though wherever we taste the water it is salty, even so, beloved, the separate self dissolves in the sea of pure consciousness, infinite and immortal.

> \- Brihadaranyaka Upanishad 2:4.12, p.38.

Love the Lord of Love and be free. He is the One
Who appears as many, enveloping
The cosmos, without beginning or end,
None but the pure in heart can realize him.

> \- Shvetashvatara Upanishad V:13, p.229.

If you become a spirit, it is the spirit which will be joined to you.

- Gospel of Philip (WI) 120.

The Soul must remove from itself good and evil and everything else, that it may receive the One alone, as the One alone. When the Soul is so blessed, and is come to it, or rather when it manifests its presence, when the Soul turns away from visible things and makes itself as beautiful as possible and becomes like the One... and seeing the One suddenly appearing in itself, for there is nothing between, nor are they any longer two, but one... it is that union of which earthly lovers, who wish to blend their being with each other, is a copy.

- Plotinus, *The Enneads* VI, 7, 34, p.135.

Without doubt, if we empty ourselves of all that belongs to the creature, depriving ourselves of all that belongs to the creature, depriving ourselves of it for the love of God, that same Lord will fill us with Himself.

- St Teresa Avila, *The Interior Castle*,
"The Seventh Mansions", 2:9

If this fusion happens, it happens quickly. The process of purification/detraumatization of the soul may take years but the fusion doesn't. It takes moments.

So mysterious is the secret and so sublime the favor that God thus bestows instantaneously on the soul

- St Teresa Avila, *The Interior Castle*,
"The Seventh Mansions", 2:3

110

Once it happens, the fusion is permanent but the sensation of fusion is temporary:

> For even though the soul is always in this sublime state of spiritual marriage once God has placed her in it, the faculties are not always in actual union although the substance is... [The] union of the faculties... is not, nor can be, continuous in this life.
>
> - St John of the Cross, *The Spiritual Canticle*, 26:11, p. 577.

The fusion of the soul with the Holy Spirit creates a once-in-eternity radiant and radiating glow. This glow fades. Just as welding two metals together requires heat but, quickly, the heat of this metallic fusion fades but the metals remain joined. After baptism by the Holy Spirit, you will wake up the next morning, feeling like you do every morning - except perhaps a bit disappointed that you cannot dwell in that radiant energy for the rest of your earthly life. Though the radiance fades, the fusion is permanent.

Nowadays we are much more familiar with the concept of things fusing. We fuse things by welding and by electro-plating. We now know that molecules can fuse together. The concept of fusion did not come so easily in ancient times. Hence, Jesus's analogy of yeast and bread.

Popular among mystics has been the image of water merging with water so that the two can never again be separated:

> ...spiritual marriage is like rain falling from heaven into a river or stream, becoming one and the same liquid so that the river and rain water cannot be divided; or it resembles a streamlet

flowing into the ocean, which cannot afterwards
be disunited from it.

> - St Teresa Avila, *The Interior Castle*,
> "The Seventh Mansions", 2:5

The Upanishads use identical analogies:

> As pure water poured into pure water
> Becomes the very same, so does the Self
> Of the illumined man or woman, Nachiketa,
> Verily become one with the Godhead
>
> > - Katha Upanishad II, 1:15, p.92.

> The flowing river is lost in the sea;
> The illumined sage is lost in the Self.
> The flowing river has become the sea;
> The illumined sage has become the Self.
>
> > - Mundaka Upanishad III, 2:8, p.117.

This metaphor of union with water was also used by John the Baptist: referring to the union of soul and spirit as "**baptism** by the Holy Spirit". But John also identifies baptism-by-Spirit as being more energetically dynamic than baptism by water: it is baptism by fire (Matt 3:11).

The Gospel of Philip (47) uses the analogy of dying cloth as an image for how the Spirit permeates and forever changes the soul:

> God is a dyer. Just as the good pigments which
> are called permanent then label the things which
> have been dyed in them, so it is with those whom
> God has colored. Because his hues are
> imperishable, (those who are tinted) become
> immortal through his hand's coloring.

Writing in a technologically more advanced era (the 16th Century), St John of the Cross tries the image of the fusion of light with glass:

> ...the two become one, as we would say of the window united with the ray of sunlight, or the coal with the fire, or the starlight with the light of the sun.
>
> - St John of the Cross, *The Spiritual Canticle* 26:4, p. 575.

Throughout the ages, people have always understood sex and marriage as powerful joinings. This analogy of male joining with female has been favored by mystics. The virgin bride (the purified soul) joins with Bridegroom (the Holy Spirit). St Teresa of Avila described it as "...Spiritual Marriage of the Bridegroom with your soul" (*The Interior Castle*, "The Seventh Mansions", 1:1). St John of the Cross describes it in identical language:

> The soul possesses all these traits, and it is necessary for her to possess them in order to reach this union with her Bridegroom...
>
> - *The Spiritual Canticle* 34:5, p. 606. [24]

The Bridegroom is the Holy Spirit:

> This flame of love is the Spirit of its Bridegroom, who is the Holy Spirit.
>
> - St John of the Cross, *The Living Flame of Love* 1:3, p. 641.

The soul fusing with the Holy Spirit is a recurring theme in the Gospel of Philip where there is talk of "Pure Mating" (64) and "Immaculate Marriage" (131). The result of the joining is a "Son".

---

[24] See Appendix Three: Sexing spirituality.

A horse naturally begets a horse, a human begets (a) human, a god begets (a) god. Thus it is regarding the Bridegroom within the Bride – [their Sons] came forth in the Bridal-Chamber. (108)

...contemplate the Pure Mating, for it has [great] power... (64)

If it is appropriate to tell a mystery, the Father of the totality mated with the Virgin who had come down – and a fire shone for him on that day. He revealed the power of the Bridal-Chamber. Thus his body came into being on that day. He came forth in the Bridal-Chamber as one who has issued from the Bridegroom with the Bride – this is how Yeshua established the totality for himself in his heart. (89)

In using a sexual image to convey the joining of the soul with the Holy Spirit, the writer of the Gospel of Philip is following the lead of Jesus who used the analogy of a virgin to describe the purified soul:

Then the kingdom of heaven will be like ten virgins who took their lamps and went to meet the bridegroom. Five of them were foolish, and five were wise. For when the foolish took their lamps, they took no oil with them, but the wise took flasks of oil with their lamps. As the bridegroom was delayed, they all became drowsy and slept. But at midnight there was a cry, "Here is the bridegroom! Come out to meet him." Then all those virgins rose and trimmed their lamps. And the foolish said to the wise, "Give us some of your oil, for our lamps are going out." But the wise answered, saying, "Since there will not be enough for us and for you, go rather to the dealers and buy for yourselves." And while they were going to buy, the bridegroom came, and those who were ready went in with him to the marriage feast, and the door was shut. Afterward the other virgins came also, saying, "Lord, lord, open to us." But he answered, "Truly, I say to you, I do not know you." Watch therefore, for you know neither the day nor the hour.

- Matthew 25:1-13

Notice that there are many virgins (purified souls) but only one bridegroom (Holy Spirit) for the divine marriage.

For this union to happen, patience is required. The soul cannot force this union to happen; it has to keep working on purification/detraumatization. You have to be patient. Jesus urges his disciples to keep their spirits up.

In a similar way, the Gospel of Philip (131) says: "No [one will be able] to know on what day [the man] and the woman mate with each other, except themselves only."

Jesus counsels the disciples to be patient and alert and ready for the coming of the Holy Spirit into their soul.

"Stay dressed for action and keep your lamps burning, and be like men who are waiting for their master to come home from the wedding feast, so that they may open the door to him at once when he comes and knocks. Blessed are those servants whom the master finds awake when he comes."

- Luke 12:35-37

Elsewhere, Jesus complains about people being impatient and trying to violently force some sort of connection with God or the divine.

"From the days of John the Baptist until now the
kingdom of heaven has suffered violence, and the
violent take it by force."
                              - Matthew 11:12

Jesus is here talking about other disciples of John the Baptist –
and perhaps some of his own as well – who mistakenly thought they
could force the union of the soul and the Holy Spirit. I think of this
passage when I hear of the terrible violence Christian devotees
would inflict on themselves over the coming centuries in an effort
to force something to happen: mortification of the flesh, celibacy,
walling themselves up, starving themselves. Such attempts at
forcing may prove counter-productive as it could indicate that the
person was consumed by an ego-driven desire which means they
are not "empty" enough to fuse with the Holy Spirit. Meister Eckhart
makes the same point – that one can be too fanatically attached to
external practices and one needs to be prepared to let go of that
attachment – even if it means breaking a vow. The enslavement to
anything can get in the way:

> All works and pious practices – praying, reading
> singing, vigils, fasting, penance, or whatever
> discipline it may be – these were invented to
> catch a man and restrain him from things alien
> and ungodly.... But if a man knows himself to be
> well trained in true inwardness, then let him
> boldly drop all outward disciplines...
> This is easy to prove, for one should consider the
> fruits and the inward truth rather than the
> outward act.
>
> - Meister Eckhart, *Complete Mystical
> Works of Meister Eckhart*, Sermon
> Three, pp. 53-4.

The coming of God into the kingdom

But wait, there's more...

Through this moment of divine fusion, the soul is now forever fused to the underlying universal energy of the Holy Spirit.

But the Holy Spirit also runs through God.

Because of this, when the soul fuses to the Holy Spirit, God the Father is able to connect to the soul via the Holy Spirit. And so it is that a transformed soul becomes not "God" but it becomes part of *the kingdom of God* – a domain through which God can potentially experience and, indeed, potentially give directions and, indeed, potentially enter into.

The kingdom of God has come.

The kingdom of God has come on Earth.

The kingdom of God has come on Earth within an individual soul.

> Thy kingdom come.
> Thy will be done in earth, as it is in heaven.
> - Matthew 6:9-10 (KJV)

First, the kingdom of God has to come within the soul: *Thy kingdom come.* The soul must first be fused to the Holy Spirit.

Only then, after this coming, can his will can be done on Earth: *Thy will be done in earth, as it is in heaven.* After the kingdom has come, the soul has the capacity to serve as an instrument of the divine on Earth. Likewise, *The Upanishads* say that, once the unification takes place, it opens up new possibilities for divine will:

> When all these three are seen as one, the Self
> Reveals his universal form and serves
> As an instrument of the divine will.
> - Shvetashvatara Upanishad 1:9, p.218.

And all these possibilities lie within you.

Whether you are a prostitute or the Pope...

Within you.

The Son of Man

Jesus sometimes referred to himself as "Son of Man":

> The Son of Man came eating and drinking, and
> they say, 'Look at him! A glutton and a drunkard,
> a friend of tax collectors and sinners!'
> > - Matthew 11:19

Jesus's other two unique coinages "the kingdom of God" and "the Holy Spirit" came directly from John the Baptist. Accordingly, we have to suspect that the expression "Son of Man" also originated with John and that (as Jesus would do after him), when alone with his disciples, John the Baptist referred to himself as a "Son of Man". Not "Son of God" but "Son of Man".

What is a son? A son is an offspring, a product of the union of two things. It is not the entities themselves but rather something that is produced by and from the union of two entities. A "Son of Man" is the offspring of the union of the Holy Spirit with the soul of a man or woman. Anyone can become a Son of Man; it is not limited to one person:

> When you can make the two into one, you
> become sons of man.
> > - Gospel of Thomas, 106. Translation by
> > Stephen J. Patterson and James M.
> > Robinson.

> ...the Holy Spirit... her children are many.
> > - Gospel of Philip 40 (WI)

> Beware that no-one lead you astray saying Lo
> here or lo there! For the Son of Man is within you.
> - Gospel of Mary 34, p. 294

The soul's baptism-by-Spirit can only come about in the body of a man or woman. Discarnate souls cannot do it. This is a marvel: that the greatest spiritual breakthrough in the universe can only take place in the body of a naked ape.

> Jesus said, "If the flesh came into being because
> of spirit, that is a marvel, but if spirit came into
> being because of the body, that is a marvel of
> marvels."
> - Gospel of Thomas, 29

To emphasize emphatically: this transformation of the soul can *only* take place in a human body. It cannot take place in "heaven" after you die. It has to take place while you are alive.

> Those who say that first they shall die and (then)
> they shall arise are confused. If they do not first
> receive the resurrection (while) they live, they
> will receive nothing (when) they die
> - Gospel of Philip, 97.

This turns upside down the denigration of the body that has gone on in so many spiritual and religious traditions throughout the centuries. It is the body that holds out the possibility of being a spiritual temple. It is the body that can become a "Bridal Chamber" in which the soul and Holy Spirit can join.

> (Paul claims that) "flesh [and blood will not be
> able] to inherit the Sovereignty [Kingdom of
> God]."[25] ... Yet this is rather what *will* inherit... I
> myself rebuke those others who say that (the

---

[25] "...flesh and blood cannot inherit the kingdom of God" (1 Corinthians 15:50)

119

flesh) shall not arise... It is necessary to arise in
this flesh, (as) everything exists within it.
- Gospel of Philip, 25

A "Son of Man" is a soul which has experienced Baptism by the Holy Spirit: the Holy Spirit and the soul of a Man/Woman have united to produce an offspring – a Son of Man.

Entering the kingdom of God

We are now in a position to better explain why John the Baptist coined the term "the kingdom of God" and why Jesus sometimes talked in terms of "entering the kingdom of God".

"Truly, I say to you, whoever does not receive the
kingdom of God like a child shall not enter it."
- Mark 10:15[26]

This is what happens during baptism by the Holy Spirit – the soul both receives the Holy Spirit and enters into the kingdom of God. Prior to baptism by the Holy Spirit, souls are effectively separate from God. God cannot connect to them but with Baptism by the Holy Spirit, all sorts of new possibilities emerge.

Recall the parable of the computer that fused with the universal Wi-Fi field. By fusing with that Wi-Fi field, the computer entered into another dimension: a dimension that is dominated by a SuperComputer of unearthly power (God). The earthly computer has entered into the SuperComputer's domain (the kingdom of God). Now, via the field of Wi-Fi vibrations (the Holy Spirit), the SuperComputer (God) can connect with the earthly computer (a Son of Man): communicate with it, access its data, instruct it. The

---

[26] Other passages making reference to entering the kingdom of God/heaven include Mark 9:47, 10:23-25; Matt 5:20, 7:21, 21:31, 23:13; Luke 18:17, 18:24-25; John 3:4-5.

SuperComputer can experience what is happening inside the earthly computer.

Let us explore this via another parable...

The Parable of the Earthly Cities

There is a great landmass...

On this landmass, there resides a powerful King. Dotted throughout this landmass are a huge number of independent cities with great walls around them. The King, as powerful as he may be, cannot penetrate these walls. He does not know what is going on behind the walls. He cannot communicate through the walls nor see what is going on inside the walls. He wants to see what is going on inside them because he thinks, apart from anything else, he can learn from what's happening in there.

But there is a way forward...

If the denizens inside one of the walled cities wanted it and worked diligently at it, they could demolish the walls and merge the walls back into the landmass from which they came. In so doing, the city becomes part of the domain of the King. The King can now access what was once isolated and impenetrable. He can sense what is going on. He can learn from that.

The huge landmass is the Holy Spirit.

The King is God.

The cities... the souls.

Just as this King could access a city if its walls were demolished, God the Father can access a transformed, baptized-by-spirit soul. A transformed soul has entered into the domain of God.

> "Truly, truly, I say to you, unless one is born of water and the Spirit, he cannot enter the kingdom of God."
>
> - John 3:5

Recall that Jesus and John the Baptist thought that this was an entirely new phenomenon – that, for the first time in all eternity, souls could be baptized by the Holy Spirit and so enter into God's kingdom. In their minds, this had become possible because the kingdom of God had drawn near to man so that souls could enter into it and this was the revolutionary good news which Jesus preached:

> "The kingdom of God has come near to you."
>
> - Luke 10:9

Is your head spinning yet?

If you are having difficulties wrapping your head around the story so far... take some consolation... it will get better... or so I believe...

You may want to re-read. You are certainly advised to re-read it sooner or later. And perhaps you are now beginning to understand why Jesus despaired of explaining this to illiterate peasants and so just spoke in parables except to his disciples who were doing the inner work. The disciples had a chance to realize the kingdom of God within their souls in their lifetimes. If they did the inner work, the expressions "the kingdom of God", "the Holy Spirit", "baptism by the Holy Spirit" would stop being just words. And Jesus promised his disciples that if they did do the inner work and stuck at it, some of them would get there.

"But I tell you truly, there are some standing here who will not taste death until they see the kingdom of God."

- Luke 9:27

The Down and Dirty Soul

You may have noticed that every mystic emphasizes that the soul has to be purified, that it has to be made as it once was, that it has to go back to what it was at the beginning. In modern terms, we would say that the soul has to be detraumatized. Analogies that mystics use for a detraumatized soul are "virgin" or "baby".

This raises a particularly interesting question: *What the hell went wrong?*

Why does spiritual progress consist in reverting the soul *back* to what it was??

Why does spiritual progress involve *going backwards*???

Fully answering these questions would take us beyond the scope of this current book and will be addressed in *The Crucifixion Code*.

The one true path

There is only one mystic path. There is only one path of true spiritual evolution. There is only one way to baptism by Spirit and so becoming a "Son of Man". There is only one path of blessedness:

1. Mourning
2. Humility (Meekness)
3. Hunger and thirst for inner rightness
4. Mercy
5. Purification (detraumatization) occasioning visions
6. Further purification occasioning the making of Peace in your soul

7. Baptism-by-Spirit (and so the soul enters into the kingdom of God)

Visions and feelings of ecstasy or ineffable Peace (stages 5 and 6) are all very nice but they are only steps along the path. St Teresa of Avila insightfully described these as "betrothal" rather than actual marriage.[27]

The path must culminate in baptism-by-Spirit or it is unfulfilled. This is the Divine Marriage that cannot be annulled.

After union of the soul with Spirit, you still keep your humanness. You are, more than ever before, a unique individual. A tremendous amount of spiritual damage has been done to people under the belief that they have to force themselves to become a clone of their perceived image of Buddha or Jesus or some other spiritual leader. Each of us is too individual for that. John the Baptist and Jesus were very different people. Jesus did not seek to make himself into a clone of his teacher:

> "For John came neither eating nor drinking, and they say, 'He has a demon.' The Son of Man came eating and drinking, and they say, 'Look at him! A glutton and a drunkard, a friend of tax collectors and sinners!' Yet wisdom is justified by her deeds."
>
> - Matthew 11:18-19

Jesus had zero interest in living up to people's image of what a holy man or prophet should be like. If he'd wanted to live up to the common conception of his day, he would not have consorted with tax collectors and prostitutes. He would not have gone anywhere near lepers.

---

[27] See Teresa of Avila, *The Interior Castle, The Seventh Mansions, Chapter II, 3-5.*

I am increasingly inclining to the opinion that the more someone apes whatever is the image of a "holy man", the less likely it is that they are one. Think about all those Christian preachers in the US who expound their myopic conception of Christian "morality" and then, over time, are exposed as adulterers and hypocrites.

Did John the Baptist ape the official holy men of his time?

Did Jesus ape the clothes and lifestyle of John the Baptist?

Speaking in tongues

It is a jungle in there: soul, Holy Spirit, Inner Child, the body with all its urges...

Within you are many voices. Many parts.

Among many things, I have studied hypnotherapy and Voice Dialogue. Using these techniques, a therapist can quickly find himself talking to a 6-year-old boy in a 42-year-old's body. Some part of the subject's psyche is still six years old.

Baptism-by-Spirit opens up the possibility that a "Son of Man" can access very distant memories of their journey as a soul. It opens up the possibility that something of a high spiritual order can speak via that person. This is something which Jesus seems to have allowed to happen in private. He never did it in public. It is something that was reserved for the disciples alone. This is assuredly the explanation behind some of the more out-there things that Jesus is recorded as saying: it was not the human part of him talking but a high spiritual part connected to the human Jesus talking via his baptized-by-Spirit soul.

> Judas (not Iscariot) said to him, "Lord, how is it
> that you will manifest yourself to us, and not to
> the world?"
>
> - John 14:22.

"To you has been given the secret of the kingdom of God, but for those outside everything is in parables; so they may indeed see but not perceive, and may indeed hear but not understand."

...With many such parables he spoke the word to them... but privately to his own disciples he explained everything.

- Mark 4:11-12, 33-34.

This is where one has to be very careful in understanding certain things that Jesus said *in private*. Some of the time, he is not talking as his human self but rather allowing something to talk via him – the Holy Spirit or perhaps even God the Father.

The words that you're hearing me say are not mine, but come from the Father...

- John 14:24 (ISV)

This is the reason why many statements attributed to Jesus in the Gospel of John need to be treated very circumspectly.

"I am the way, and the truth and the life; no-one comes to the Father but by me."

- John 14:6.

This is NOT Jesus's human self talking. If it is accurate to what came from Jesus's lips, this was the Holy Spirit talking via Jesus's baptized soul. If so, it is accurate: the Holy Spirit is the way to the Father.

Jesus said, "I am the light that is over all things. I am all: from me all came forth, and to me all attained. Split a piece of wood; I am there. Lift up the stone, and you will find me there."

- Gospel of Thomas 77

Again, this cannot be considered to be the human Jesus talking. It is a high spiritual part (the Holy Spirit) speaking via the human Jesus's mouth. Jesus indicates that this ability to let the Holy Spirit talk via the individual's voice is something that others could one day achieve including his disciples:

> "And when they bring you before the synagogues and the rulers and the authorities, do not be anxious about how you should defend yourself or what you should say, for the Holy Spirit will teach you in that very hour what you ought to say."
> - Luke 12:11-12

Jesus Delusion #5

The Virgin Mary

Of all the out-there ideas that have clustered around the figure of Jesus, there may be none more absurd than that of the Virgin Mary: that Jesus was born of a virgin.

But wait, there's more...

You have probably heard of the doctrine of the "Immaculate Conception" and perhaps vaguely thought that it applied to Jesus: that he was immaculately conceived. No, no. The doctrine of the Immaculate Conception – still held as a central tenet by the Roman Catholic Church – applies to Mary and holds that she was born free of the Original Sin which all humans are heir to – apart from her and Jesus. For how could the divine Jesus have come from a woman who was in the slightest way tainted by sin or (horror of horrors) sex?

The most historically reliable and earliest of the Gospels, the Gospel of Mark, has no reference to anything special about the birth of Jesus. The first and last time his mother makes an appearance is when Jesus starts preaching. Mary and her other children hear about this and think Jesus must have lost the plot, if not his mind (Mark 3:21).

The later Gospels of Matthew and Luke include what surely started as an oral tale: that Jesus was born of a virgin. This fable was framed so that Jesus could appear to be the fulfillment of an Old Testament prophecy:

> Therefore the Lord himself shall give you a sign;
> Behold, a virgin shall conceive, and bear a son,
> and shall call his name Immanuel.
> - Isaiah 7:14

This is yet another unfulfilled prediction because Jesus was never referred to as "Immanuel" in his lifetime but called "Yeshua" (his given name) or "Rabbi" (Teacher).

Moreover, this translation of Isaiah is very dubious. The original Hebrew word was "*almah*" which means "young woman who has not yet had a baby" (she may or may not have been deflowered). When it was translated into the Greek Septuagint (completed in the late 2nd Century BC), the translators chose to translate "*almah*" with the Greek word "*parthenos*" which does mean "virgin". Well that imprecise translation has had titanic theological consequences that the original translators could have never foreseen.

When the landmark Revised Standard Version of the Bible came out in 1952, it translated "*almah*" as "young woman" instead of "virgin". That translation became an instant controversy.

This passage from Isaiah is specifically trotted out in the Gospel of Matthew (1:22-23) as having been fulfilled by Jesus. What the authors of the Gospels of Matthew and Luke could have never foreseen is how Mary would become a cult unto herself. Indeed, in some places, it seems like the cult of the Virgin Mary is bigger than the cult of Jesus.

Is there some deep-seated psycho-spiritual explanation for this level of devotion to the Virgin Mary?

I think there is.

We have begun our exploration of the writings of mystics. We have seen that they talk about the need a soul has to be made pure. The analogy that repeatedly comes up is that of a virgin or a virgin bride – one that is ready for union with the "Holy Spirit" – and this union results in a divine birth.

Very interestingly, unlike Greek mythic figures, Mary is not portrayed as being impregnated by God or a god but by the Holy

Spirit (Matt 1:18; Luke 1:34-35). The Virgin Mary provides a near-perfect (if unconscious) symbol for the "virgin" purified soul ready to receive the Holy Spirit and so give birth to a "Son".

The historical Mary was not a virgin. But the Virgin Mary as symbol holds the power and appeal of what is needed on the spiritual path: a "pure" soul through which a Son of the Holy Spirit can be "born".

Indeed, the idea of Jesus having been born of a virgin could have had its point of origin in things Jesus said privately to his disciples. In one of his parables, Jesus uses the metaphorical image of virgin brides waiting for the bridegroom (Matt 25:1-13). This is actually a pretty common image among mystics for the "Divine Marriage" (baptism by the Holy Spirit): a purified "virgin" soul joins with the "bridegroom" of the Holy-Spirit/Brahman/The-One and thereby a "Son of Man" is created. After Jesus's death, this simile seems to have become transubstantiated into Jesus having actually been born of a human virgin (Mary) with the Holy Spirit as bridegroom.

Probably only a behind-the-scenes scenario such as this can explain why Jesus was enshrined as being the result of the union of a Virgin Bride with the mysterious Holy Spirit whereas the standard model across the Mediterranean was to have a special person born of sex between a god and a woman (e.g., Hercules, Achilles, Perseus, etc).

What of the real Mary and her actual relationship with her son?

If one looks critically at the Gospels, apart from the ridiculous nativity scenes, one is forced to consider that Jesus's relationship with his actual mother was not that close – and perhaps not good at all.

In the Gospel of Mark, Mary is totally in the dark about Jesus's spiritual work. She goes out with her other sons to stage an intervention, thinking he'd gone crazy (Mark 3:20). Apparently, Jesus had not told them anything about going into the wilderness nor about his time with John the Baptist. When Jesus is told that his family is outside wanting to see him, he shows no compunction about totally ignoring them (Mark 3:33-35). In this Gospel of Mark – the most credible in terms of the events in Jesus's life – this is the one and only appearance of his mother.

This theme of a lack of respect from his relatives is taken up again later in the Gospel of Mark when, as part of his ministry, Jesus calls into his small hometown of Nazareth and receives a cynical and hostile reception.

> He went away from there and came to his hometown, and his disciples followed him. And on the Sabbath he began to teach in the synagogue, and many who heard him were astonished, saying, "Where did this man get these things? What is the wisdom given to him? How are such mighty works done by his hands? Is not this the carpenter, the son of Mary and brother of James and Joses and Judas and Simon? And are not his sisters here with us?" And they took offense at him. And Jesus said to them, "A prophet is not without honor, except in his hometown and among his relatives and in his own household."
> - Mark 6:1-4

The Gospel of Luke (4:29) paints his reception as far worse even than this – the hometown locals want to throw him off a cliff as a false prophet.

One inevitable conclusion from this is that, as a child and youth, there was nothing special about Jesus that might have caused his neighbors or relatives to earmark him for remarkable things.

Moreover, after their earlier attempt to confront Jesus, obviously his mother and brothers had not started boasting to the neighbors about Jesus and his ministry. He was "without honor" among his relatives.

Also note that Jesus came from what seems, by present-day standards, to be a large family. He had four brothers and at least two sisters. This means that, at most, there was only one chance in seven that he was the oldest child. If there were five boys then, under the law of averages, there could well have been five girls. At least some of the sisters were still in Nazareth at the time of his visit. As the brothers are not mentioned as still being in Nazareth, they may have been off in other parts of the country where there would have been more work to be found. Tellingly, there is no mention here of Jesus attempting to visit his parents or sisters when in Nazareth nor any attempt by them to see him.

The Gospel of Luke (2:41-45) recounts a disturbing incident where, when Jesus was 12, this substantial family group went up to Jerusalem for the Passover. After it, the family starts the long trip back to Nazareth. For a full day, his parents do not even notice that Jesus is not with them and is still back in Jerusalem! Shades of the film *Home Alone* where the youngest child is accidentally left behind. On the basis of this incident, you would have to think that Jesus was not the eldest son as it is less likely that parents would lose track of the most prized child. This incident also indicates a lack of affection from Jesus towards his family – he would rather be at the Temple than with them.

Decades later, in his teachings, Jesus says that unless someone hates his mother and father, they cannot be his disciple (Luke 14:16). This also indicates that Jesus had issues with his own parents.

Jesus also warns that his teachings are not going to bring families together but rip them apart "father against son and son against father, mother against daughter and daughter against mother" (Luke 12:53). Again, this indicates that his own family was not reconciled to his ministry.

The letters of the Apostle Paul state that, after his death, Jesus appeared to his brother James (1 Corinthians 15:3-8). But there is no Gospel that claims that the resurrected Jesus appeared to his mother, his father or his other siblings. This indicates some fondness for his brother James but no emotional connection to the rest of his family

Oh but, at his crucifixion, wasn't his mother devotedly there, watching on in horror? Her presence is recorded only in the Gospel of John – by far the most historically unreliable of the Gospels. The other Gospels list women followers as being at the Crucifixion – even mentioning some of them by name such as Mary Magdalene – but with no mention of his mother (Mark 15:40, Matt 27:56, Luke 23:49).

On the basis of the Gospel of Mark, it seems that his family had effectively disowned Jesus and wanted nothing to do with this radical preacher.

The unavoidable conclusion of all this is that Jesus did not have some idealized relationship with a sanctified mother and a perfect father but rather had substantial issues with his imperfect earthly parents and flawed siblings.

And, in this, he is exactly like the rest of us.

Jesus Delusion #6

The Virgin Jesus

Only marginally less strange than the delusion of the Virgin Mary is the delusion of the Virgin Jesus. Faith-based Christians seem strangely devoted to the idea that Jesus was a virgin.

Let us look at the actual Gospels:

- In no Gospel does it state that Jesus was a virgin
- In no Gospel does Jesus ask his disciples to be celibate
- In no Gospel does Jesus recommend virginity or celibacy
- In no Gospel does Jesus condemn sex or even prostitution. Indeed, there is a famous incident in the modern version of the Gospel of John, where he defends a prostitute (John 8:1-11). "Let he who is without sin cast the first stone."

How did Christianity ever come to trumpet the idea of celibate priests? How did Christianity develop this bizarre obsession against sexuality? How is it that so many Christians are so deeply attached to the idea of a Virgin Jesus?

Think about this: Would you take life advice from a virgin? From someone who had never been in relationship? Never loved?

What would such a person know about real life?

So how did Christianity become so anti-sex?

Part of the blame lies with the Apostle Paul. Paul was convinced that the Apocalypse was coming any day now. As such, it was logical for him to oppose people having children. You could only be saved by having faith in Jesus. Babies were too young to have faith in Jesus therefore they would not be saved during the Apocalypse. Therefore, the best course was to not have sex and not have babies.

As was the case with the Virgin Mary, part of the blame may lie with our unconscious psycho-spiritual prejudices. We instinctively sense the need for a "pure" soul. We unconsciously feel that somehow the body "dirties" the soul so that the only way a soul can be truly pure is to reject all bodily things.

In terms of the real mystic path, this psycho-spiritual prejudice against the body is nonsense. The soul actually needs to incarnate in order to evolve, in order to be detraumatized and made pure. To re-quote Meister Eckhart:

> ...the soul is given to the body in order to be purified.
>
> - Meister Eckhart, *Selected Writings*, pp.167-8.

Release the ludicrous attachment to the idea of a Virgin Jesus. Instead, accept that he had a full rich life and he went through the journey of the body... a body that shits, farts, gets sick, ages and, yes, orgasms and has sex.

And such a body is necessary to spiritually evolve.

Part V

The Death of the Covenant

"Every tree that does not bear good fruit is cut down and thrown into the fire."

- Matthew 7:19

The people of the covenant

John the Baptist and Jesus were Jews.

As such, they were raised into the belief that they were members of a special people singled out by God. Unlike every other tribe and nation, the Israelites had a covenant with the one true God. It started with Abraham:

> "Behold, my covenant is with you, and you shall be the father of a multitude of nations. No longer shall your name be called Abram, but your name shall be Abraham, for I have made you the father of a multitude of nations... And I will give to you and to your offspring after you the land of your sojournings, all the land of Canaan, for an everlasting possession, and I will be their God."
> And God said to Abraham, "As for you, you shall keep my covenant, you and your offspring after you throughout their generations. This is my covenant, which you shall keep, between me and you and your offspring after you: Every male among you shall be circumcised. You shall be circumcised in the flesh of your foreskins, and it shall be a sign of the covenant between me and you."
>
> - Genesis 17:4-9

Later this covenant would undergo an incredibly detailed clarification via Moses:

> "Now therefore, if you will indeed obey my voice and keep my covenant, you shall be my treasured possession among all peoples, for all the earth is

> mine; and you shall be to me a kingdom of priests
> and a holy nation."
>
>   - Exodus 19:5-6

The Mosaic Law laid out exactly what hoops Israelites had to jump through to keep up their end of the covenant: they had to keep the Ten Commandments and a huge list of other Laws. As far as the Israelites were concerned, this covenant with God made them the most special nation on Earth.

And, arguably, they were.

The Israelites were the flag-bearers for monotheism – for the belief in the One God. Pretty much everyone else in the known world was a pagan with a pantheon of gods. Only Judaism had the One True God. It was this idea of monotheism that would come to dominate the world via Christianity and Islam.

When Jesus sends out his twelve disciples to preach, he instructs them:

> "Go nowhere among the Gentiles and enter no
> town of the Samaritans, but go rather to the lost
> sheep of the house of Israel."
>
>   - Matthew, 10:5-6.

It was not worth their while preaching to the Gentiles. Why? First, because the Gentiles did not believe in One God. If Israelites were struggling to understand "the coming of the kingdom of God" then how were pagan Gentiles – who believed in an army of gods – going to wrap their heads around this idea?

Second, it is also quite possible that both John the Baptist and Jesus believed that *only* Israelites were capable of realizing the kingdom of God – i.e., experiencing baptism by the Holy Spirit. For them, this was a new blessing that was being bestowed upon Israelites – the true believers, the people of the covenant, the chosen nation of the One God. Why would the One God be drawing closer to Gentiles who did not even believe in him? With whom he had no covenant?

> ...a woman whose little daughter had an unclean spirit heard of him and came and fell down at his feet. Now the woman was a Gentile, a Syrophoenician by birth. And she begged him to cast the demon out of her daughter. And he said to her, "Let the children be fed first, for it is not right to take the children's bread and throw it to the dogs." But she answered him, "Yes, Lord; yet even the dogs under the table eat the children's crumbs." And he said to her, "For this statement you may go your way; the demon has left your daughter." And she went home and found the child lying in bed and the demon gone.
>
> - Mark 7:25-30

To Jesus and John the Baptist, Gentiles were ultimately, in a sense, on the same spiritual level as animals. Unlike the Israelites, the Gentiles were not in relationship with the One God. How then could Gentiles possibly experience baptism by the Holy Spirit??

John and Jesus had no knowledge of the ancient Indian texts of *The Upanishads*. If these texts had been available to them, they would have recognized something of their own experiences in them and the Jewish-centeredness of what they taught would have faded... presumably...

The death of the Israelite hierarchy

One of the puzzles of the Biblical Gospels is: Why was the Jewish religious hierarchy so upset with Jesus?

He was just a preacher wandering around the countryside, talking up the value of inner spiritual growth, recommending that people be good and forgive others. Why would that get up the noses of the religious hierarchy?

A key part of the answer is: because they were a hierarchy. The hierarchy was partly inherited and partly a meritocracy – you could get merit from such things as learning and piety and increasing your wealth or power. For instance, King David rose from being a shepherd boy.

There was a priestly class and you had to be born into it: to be eligible, you had to be a descendent of Aaron, the brother of Moses. To get to the very top of the heap, the office of High Priest, you were traditionally supposed to be a descendent of Zadok, the first High Priest of the First Temple.

The Israelites basically had "a great chain of spiritual being". At the top was God and then under him seraphim and cherubim and archangels and angels. At the very bottom were the unclean: the lepers, the prostitutes. Indeed, if you were a Samaritan or a Gentile, you were lower than the bottom. This Great Chain of Spiritual Being was enshrined into everyday Israelite life. You would not break bread and eat with someone significantly below you. This Jewish Great Chain of Spiritual Being was probably something like this:

God

Angels

Past Prophets

The High Priest

King (if there was one – noting that Kings were supposed to get the approval of God)

Senior priests

Sadducees (who generally came from the wealthy class)

Scribes (Pharisees came in at around this level)

Land-owners

Merchants

Manual workers like Jesus

Tax collectors for the Romans

Women

The unclean (prostitutes, lepers, homeless, menstruating women, etc.)

Samaritans

Gentiles

Following in the footsteps of John the Baptist, Jesus threw the hierarchy out the window. He drank and feasted with tax collectors and prostitutes. He said that a Samaritan could be better than a priest - remember the parable of the Good Samaritan.

> And when he was demanded of the Pharisees, when the kingdom of God should come, he answered them and said, The kingdom of God cometh not with observation:
> Neither shall they say, Lo here! or, lo there! for, behold, the kingdom of God is within you.
> - Luke:17: 20-21 (KJV)

This is a manifesto of a spiritual revolution.

Everyone has the kingdom of God inside them. Everyone. Prostitutes. Tax collectors. Lepers. Everyone. The same.

Everyone is equal in the quest for spiritual evolution. (More exactly, every Israelite was equal in the quest for spiritual evolution.) John the Baptist and Jesus preached spiritual equality between all Israelites. Absolute spiritual democracy. Every man and every woman is born spiritually equal and has the same spiritual potential.

As such, these two preachers were the ultimate blasphemers against the Jewish religious hierarchy.

The Jewish religious hierarchy knew where the kingdom of God was and it wasn't inside any bottom-feeders like prostitutes. It was in the Holy of Holies, the most sacred spot on Earth, situated deep inside the great Temple in Jerusalem. Originally, this was where the Ark of the Covenant rested. Only the High Priest could pass through the veil which separated the Holy of Holies from the rest of the Temple. And even he could only enter one day a year. That was where the kingdom of God was on Earth. Not inside lepers and prostitutes. But Jesus was saying, "No, the Holy of Holies is inside you. It is inside everyone. From prostitutes to high priests. The same." The Gospel of Matthew records Jesus as slapping the religious hierarchy in the face when he says exactly this to the chief priests and elders in Jerusalem:

> "Truly, I say to you, the tax collectors and the prostitutes go into the kingdom of God before you. For John [the Baptist] came to you in the way of righteousness, and you did not believe him, but the tax collectors and the prostitutes believed him. And even when you saw it, you did not afterward change your minds and believe him."
> - Matthew 21:31-32.

This cannot be!

Unclean prostitutes cannot be above high priests in spiritual standing!

The Gospel of Mark reports that, at the instant of the death of Jesus, the veil separating the Holy of Holies from the rest of the world was torn from top to bottom (Mark 15:38). But the truth is that Jesus started tearing that veil from the moment he first talked about the kingdom of God. He tore asunder the illusion that the kingdom of God could be in any physical place. He ripped apart the idea that there was any sort of religious hierarchy. John the Baptist and Jesus tore the veil separating God from man.

> "I tell you, something greater than the Temple is here."
>
> - Matthew 12:6

No wonder the high priests seethed. If the kingdom of God could be realized by anyone – even the unclean – what became of the Holy of Holies? The Temple? The High Priest? The rest of the priesthood? The ritual sacrifices?

All gone.

This is why it is the most ironic of blasphemies is to make Jesus into the only begotten Son of God – divine before he was even born. It makes nonsense of the whole ministry of Jesus and John the Baptist. It reinstalls a religious hierarchy – with Jesus above us all. How can any of us possibly attain to the heights of someone already born the Son of God? Making Jesus into the eternal Son of God re-enshrined the Great Chain of Spiritual Being. This is what the Catholic Church did: making an even more set-in-stone Great Chain of Being by insisting that Jesus was born the Son of God – indeed, was the Son of God before he was even born as a man. The church's message was not the message of Jesus: *We all have the kingdom of God inside us and can realize it.* Instead the church's message was: *Only Jesus could do it. We are unworthy of him. We should just worship him.*

Worse, the Christian hierarchy then claimed greater spiritual standing than the common man and woman by the line of apostolic succession: Jesus appointed the Apostle Peter who then appointed his successor who then appointed their successors... etc.... And so it was that popes, bishops, priests were all spiritually above the common man and woman.

I am not exactly sure what Jesus would have said about this but I suspect that, being the plain speaker he was, it might have started off with something like: "You brood of vipers..."

But it wasn't just the Israelite hierarchy that John the Baptist and Jesus declared to be dead.

The Death of the Old Covenant

Does this book irritate you? Make you angry? Infuriate you?

For many faith-based Christians, this book may well be a source of massive irritation. They believe they have a covenant with God: *Obey the Ten Commandments, go to church, have faith in Jesus as your Lord and Savior and you will be rewarded: when you die, your soul will go to heaven.*

There is no such covenant. Jesus preached the opposite of that: forget about faith, go on a journey of inner spiritual evolution.

No, no, you can't take that covenant away from us. Our whole lives are based around it: Do good, Have faith, Go to heaven.

In a virtual identical way, two thousand years ago, the major source of irritation that the Jewish hierarchy had with John the Baptist and Jesus is that what they preached undercut key parts of the covenant of Moses – the covenant which promised that if Israelites obeyed the Ten Commandments and all the other minutiae of Mosaic Law [28] , then God would stay in special

---

[28] See Exodus 20-23 and even that is only part of it. Eventually it would be concluded that there were 613 commandments. See "613 Commandments" in Wikipedia.

relationship with the Israelites. John the Baptist pronounced this covenant to be superseded. This old way was not enough anymore. Not nearly enough. God now demanded more:

> "Well, then, start producing fruits in keeping with a change of heart, and don't even start saying to yourselves, 'We have Abraham for our father.' Let me tell you, God can raise up children for Abraham right out of these rocks."
>
> - Luke 3:8[29]

Jesus too was clear that John the Baptist marked a new era that superseded the era of the Law and the Prophets:

> "The Law and the Prophets were proclaimed until John. Since that time, the good news of the kingdom of God is being preached..."
>
> - Luke 16:16 (NIV)

This is the second great reason that the Jewish religious hierarchy loathed John the Baptist and Jesus: they preached the radical revision of the old covenant of Moses, the rock on which the Israelite hierarchy and subservient guilt-ridden Jewish normality were built.

The old covenant was not enough for God now. God wanted more: he wanted souls to bear fruit. He wanted souls to be baptized-by-Spirit so that God could connect to them and could experience the fruit of their journeys as souls.

Not only by his words but also by his actions, Jesus made it plain that he believed the Old Covenant was dead. He didn't strictly keep the Sabbath (Mark 2:23-27). He even said that a Son of Man was above the Sabbath: "...the Son of Man is lord even of the Sabbath" (Mark 2:28). He had no problem about eating with "defiled hands"

---

[29] Translation from Robert J. Miller (ed), *The Complete Gospels*.

(Mark 7:1-5). When challenged by the Pharisees, he is prepared to take all the ritualized actions required by the Law of Moses and throw them out the window; it is now the inner life that counts:

> For from within, out of the heart of man, come evil thoughts, sexual immorality, theft, murder, adultery, coveting, wickedness, deceit, sensuality, envy, slander, pride, foolishness. All these evil things come from within, and they defile a person.
>
> - Mark 7:21-23

When asked by a rich young man as to what steps he needed to take to be on the path to eternal life, Jesus slices the huge complexity of the Law of Moses down to this:

> "Do not murder, Do not commit adultery, Do not steal, Do not bear false witness, Do not defraud, Honor your father and mother."
>
> - Mark 10:19

That's it. Not even the entire Ten Commandments have to be obeyed. Indeed, in one place, Jesus says that even blaspheming against God is forgivable; it is blaspheming against the Holy Spirit which is not forgivable:

> "Truly, I say to you, all sins will be forgiven the children of man, and whatever blasphemies they utter, but whoever blasphemes against the Holy Spirit never has forgiveness, but is guilty of an eternal sin..."
>
> - Mark 3:28-29

Jesus would eventually be crucified under the charge of sedition against Rome. There is no doubt that the Jewish chief priests thought that Jesus should be executed for sedition – but not for sedition against Rome but for sedition against them and the covenant.

As part of John the Baptist's leapfrogging of the old covenant, there was to be a radical revision in the idea of sin and forgiveness. The whole money-making machine of the Jerusalem Temple was ultimately built on Jewish guilt. You had to come to the Temple, fork out money, pray, sing, repent, make sacrifices and that was how you got to put your transgressions in the past and come back into relationship with God. But John the Baptist and Jesus said: No. *Now there is a new way.*

> John appeared, baptizing in the wilderness and proclaiming a baptism of repentance for the forgiveness of sins. And all the country of Judea and all Jerusalem were going out to him and were being baptized by him in the river Jordan, confessing their sins.
> - Mark 1:4-5

How could this be? No expensive sacrifices? No half-shekel entry fee just to get into the Temple? Just going out into the wilderness and being baptized!? For free???

No wonder John the Baptist was popular with the people... and very unpopular with the upper hierarchy.

Worse...

John and Jesus were preaching that God would accept the worst of sinners, the most fallen of souls, the most prodigal of sons – as long as you committed to the path of inner transformation, the path of blessedness, the path of the Beatitudes. All your sinful past would not matter to God, as long as you changed your ways, transformed your soul and bore fruit for him.

Worse...

Jesus, traveling in the countryside and towns, had no easy access to the symbolic power of baptism in water so, on occasion, he would just tell people they were forgiven (e.g., Mark 2:1-11).

This was the revolution started by John the Baptist and carried forward by Jesus: the hierarchy was dead, the old covenant was superseded, old ideas about financially-burdensome forgiveness were dead.

Now there was a New Covenant.

The New Covenant: Transform your soul or else...

There was a New Covenant now: Israelites had to purify their souls until they experienced baptism by the Holy Spirit and, in so doing, make their souls part of the kingdom of God. Then they would have borne fruit which God could harvest from their journeys as souls.

As far as John the Baptist and Jesus knew, baptism of the soul by the Holy Spirit was an absolutely new phenomenon in the history of the planet. The new era wasn't coming. It was here. The kingdom of God had already arrived on earth... within the souls of John and Jesus and doubtless other disciples of John.

This was a momentous turning point in history.

> He also said to the crowds, "When you see a cloud rising in the west, you say at once, 'A shower is coming.' And so it happens. And when you see the south wind blowing, you say, 'There will be scorching heat,' and it happens. You hypocrites! You know how to interpret the appearance of earth and sky, but why do you not know how to interpret the present time?"
> - Luke 12:54-56

Union of the soul and spirit (baptism by the Holy Spirit) was not just something that God wanted from Israelites; it was something he demanded from them. The image that comes up with both John and Jesus is the bearing of fruit: souls that have been baptized-by-Spirit have borne fruit from their journey as souls, fruit which God can harvest:

> "Every tree therefore that does not bear good fruit is cut down and thrown into the fire."
> - John the Baptist, Matthew 3:10

Jesus says exactly the same thing:

> "Every tree that does not bear good fruit is cut down and thrown into the fire."
> - Matthew 7:19

Jesus also suggests that souls who have not been planted with the Holy Spirit will be ripped up.

> "Every plant that my heavenly Father has not planted will be rooted up."
> - Matthew 15:13

These are powerful claims. The time has come when souls have to bear fruit or else. God cannot reap a harvest from an unbaptized soul. An untransformed soul is a closed book to God. He cannot learn from it; he cannot relate to it; it has not borne fruit; it is useless to him. It may as well be discarded. It should be thrown in the bin.

God is coming and he is coming soon. He is coming to harvest souls who have borne fruit by being transformed, by being baptized by Spirit.

> And he said, "The kingdom of God is as if a man should scatter seed on the ground. He sleeps and

rises night and day, and the seed sprouts and grows; he knows not how. The earth produces by itself, first the blade, then the ear, then the full grain in the ear. But when the grain is ripe, at once he puts in the sickle, because the harvest has come."

- Mark 4:26-29

People – John the Baptist, Jesus and others – have transformed their souls. So the time is ripe for the harvesting of souls. If you haven't borne fruit by having your soul baptized by spirit, the best you can hope for is that you show some promise so that you will be granted more time to transform your soul and so bear fruit.

And he told this parable: "A man had a fig tree planted in his vineyard, and he came seeking fruit on it and found none. And he said to the vinedresser, 'Look, for three years now I have come seeking fruit on this fig tree, and I find none. Cut it down. Why should it use up the ground?' And he answered him, 'Sir, let it alone this year also, until I dig around it and put on manure. Then if it should bear fruit next year, well and good; but if not, you can cut it down.'"

- Luke 13:6-9

Recall Jesus's seven stages of blessedness:
1. Mourning
2. Humility
3. Hunger and thirst for inner rightness
4. Mercy
5. Purification occasioning visions
6. Further purification occasioning the making of Peace in your soul.

7. The realization of the kingdom of heaven (baptism by the Holy Spirit)

Any person can have a level of humility (meekness) and hunger for inner change and can develop greater mercy and compassion for others. This then would be evidence that they are some steps along the path toward baptism by the Holy Spirit. In so doing, such people will buy themselves extra time to get on with inner spiritual evolution. Both Jesus and John the Baptist emphasized their listeners should immediately start acting compassionately towards others and develop purity of intent.

When John the Baptist tells the crowds that "the axe is laid to the root of the tree" and that every tree that doesn't bear fruit will be thrown into the fire, the crowds ask him, "What shall we do?" (Luke 3:10) Now John knows that only a small number are hungry enough to stay on as his disciples in the wilderness so he admonishes them to take the step of mercy:

> And he answered them, "Whoever has two tunics
> is to share with him who has none, and whoever
> has food is to do likewise." Tax collectors also
> came to be baptized and said to him, "Teacher,
> what shall we do?" And he said to them, "Collect
> no more than you are authorized to do." Soldiers
> also asked him, "And we, what shall we do?" And
> he said to them, "Do not extort money from
> anyone by threats or by false accusation, and be
> content with your wages."
> - Luke 3:11-14

Likewise, Jesus admonishes people to take the vital step of compassion toward others:

> And one of the scribes came up and heard them
> disputing with one another, and seeing that he

answered them well, asked him, "Which commandment is the most important of all?" Jesus answered, "The most important is, 'Hear, O Israel: The Lord our God, the Lord is one. And you shall love the Lord your God with all your heart and with all your soul and with all your mind and with all your strength.' The second is this: 'You shall love your neighbor as yourself.' There is no other commandment greater than these." And the scribe said to him, "You are right, Teacher. You have truly said that he is one, and there is no other besides him. And to love him with all the heart and with all the understanding and with all the strength, and to love one's neighbor as oneself, is much more than all whole burnt offerings and sacrifices." And when Jesus saw that he answered wisely, he said to him, "You are not far from the kingdom of God."

- Mark 12:28-34

So what happens to the souls who don't even show mercy and purity of intent towards others? Who have bad intentions towards others? Who commit evil actions? John and Jesus suggest that they will be utterly and painfully annihilated – using the symbol of fire for this annihilation.

He put another parable before them, saying, "The kingdom of heaven may be compared to a man who sowed good seed in his field, but while his men were sleeping, his enemy came and sowed weeds among the wheat and went away. So when the plants came up and bore grain, then the weeds appeared also. And the servants of the master of the house came and said to him,

'Master, did you not sow good seed in your field? How then does it have weeds?' He said to them, 'An enemy has done this.' So the servants said to him, 'Then do you want us to go and gather them?' But he said, 'No, lest in gathering the weeds you root up the wheat along with them. Let both grow together until the harvest, and at harvest time I will tell the reapers, Gather the weeds first and bind them in bundles to be burned, but gather the wheat into my barn.'"

- Matthew 13:24-30.

"Again, the kingdom of heaven is like a net that was thrown into the sea and gathered fish of every kind. When it was full, men drew it ashore and sat down and sorted the good into containers but threw away the bad. So it will be at the close of the age. The angels will come out and separate the evil from the righteous and throw them into the fiery furnace. In that place there will be weeping and gnashing of teeth."

- Matthew 13:47-50.

In summary, John the Baptist and Jesus held these beliefs:

1. Baptism by the Holy Spirit was a revolutionary new spiritual phenomenon.

2. It was a special gift by God to the Israelite people and indicated that God was drawing closer to his chosen people. ("The kingdom of God is at hand.")

3. God the Father now demanded baptism by the Holy Spirit from every Israelite soul.

4. Israelites who did not transform their souls through union-with-Spirit would not have borne fruit for God. He could not connect to their souls and learn from their journey so

he would act to discard such souls. They had not entered into his kingdom.

5. However, you could buy yourself extra time if you showed promise that you were heading towards transformation of your soul. The key step which everyone could make was mercy towards others (forgiveness, compassion, purity of intent).

6. The hopeless cases would have their souls annihilated through the spiritual equivalent of fire. This would be a painful process.

7. It didn't matter how horrible and prodigal and even downright evil you'd been, as long as you made it far enough along the path of the Beatitudes, you'd escape annihilation. Indeed, Jesus had a problem with the idea that people who were evil could escape annihilation which is one reason he talked in parables:

> "To you has been given the secret of the kingdom of God, but for those outside everything is in parables, so that they may indeed see but not perceive, and may indeed hear but not understand, lest they should turn and be forgiven."
>
> - Mark 4:11-12.

8. And non-Israelites? Well, there was almost certainly no hope for them. They did not believe in the One God. God had not drawn closer to them. Surely, they could not even experience baptism by the Holy Spirit.

Of course, all this could happen without an apocalypse on Earth. It could just be a judgment of souls after physical death.

But something was soon going to happen to Jesus... something so momentous that he would abandon his mission of preaching the kingdom of God and come to believe that there was going to be an apocalyptic judgment of souls that would take place soon... and it would be led by not by Jesus but by a mysterious figure he called "the Son of Man". But discussion of this must wait upon the second book in this series, *The Crucifixion Code*.

So what did Jesus think happens after you die?

Let us place Jesus in the context of what Jews at the time tended to believe about the afterlife. Strangely, for such a closely bonded and strict religion, there was tremendous disagreement about what happens after death.

The Sadducees believed that there was no afterlife at all. You just died, and that was it.

The Pharisees believed that you did go on after death but there seemed to be divergent views amongst them about what form that afterlife would take:

- **Reincarnation and hell.** Josephus, the Jewish historian, was a Pharisee, and he portrays them as believing in reincarnation of good souls and eternal punishment for bad souls: "They [the Pharisees] say that all souls are incorruptible, but that the souls of good men only are removed into other bodies, - but that the souls of bad men are subject to eternal punishment."[30]

- **Resurrection of a spiritual body.** This is what the Apostle Paul, a former Pharisee, believed in: that the figure of Jesus he saw was a luminous resurrected spiritual body that

---

[30] *War of the Jews* 2.8.14 William Whiston translation. Available free at www.ccel.org. Also see the Article "Pharisees" in Wikipedia.

looked like his physical body. (To be discussed in detail in *The Crucifixion Code*.)

- **Resurrection of a physical body.** Perhaps some of the Pharisees believed in the physical resurrection of the dead. Hard to be certain but the fact that this came to be a popular opinion in the early Jesus movement tends to indicate that some Jews held it.

It also seems that at least some Jews believed in ghosts:

> As they were talking about these things, Jesus himself stood among them, and said to them, "Peace to you!" But they were startled and frightened and thought they saw a spirit.
> - Luke 24:36-37

Many Israelites believed that if you were really close to God, you didn't die – at least not in the same way that other people did. For instance, the Old Testament prophet Elijah didn't die but was taken up (2 Kings 2:9-12). Possibly similar is Enoch who walked with God and "God took" (Genesis 5:24).

So, amidst all this diversity, what did Jesus believe?

There is an incident where Jesus specifically discusses the afterlife in response to an antagonistic question from some Sadducees:

> And Sadducees came to him, who say that there is no resurrection. And they asked him a question, saying, "Teacher, Moses wrote for us that if a man's brother dies and leaves a wife, but leaves no child, the man must take the widow and raise up offspring for his brother. There were seven brothers; the first took a wife, and when he died left no offspring. And the second took her, and

died, leaving no offspring. And the third likewise. And the seven left no offspring. Last of all the woman also died. In the resurrection, when they rise again, whose wife will she be? For the seven had her as wife."

Jesus said to them, "Is this not the reason you are wrong, because you know neither the Scriptures nor the power of God? For when they rise from the dead, they neither marry nor are given in marriage, but are like angels in heaven."

- Mark 12:18-25

This is the best description we have from Jesus about what he thinks will happen to baptized-by-Spirit souls in the afterlife: they will dwell in the spiritual dimension ("heaven") just as angels do. That, of course, is also where God dwells ("Our Father which art in heaven"). Jesus then goes on to say something which sounds like he doesn't believe in physical resurrection at all:

"And as for the dead being raised, have you not read in the book of Moses, in the passage about the bush, how God spoke to him, saying, 'I am the God of Abraham, and the God of Isaac, and the God of Jacob'? He is not God of the dead, but of the living. You are quite wrong."

- Mark 12:26-27

As presumably only God would be able to physically raise people from the dead and, as God is a God of the living not the dead, this really does sound like Jesus is putting the kybosh on the whole idea of any sort of physical resurrection into this worldly plane – even though this idea would become a widespread belief in the Jesus movement.

If you die and ascend to heaven, you automatically become greater than any living person ever – even greater than the person whom Jesus rated the greatest of all, his teacher John the Baptist.

> "Truly, I say to you, among those born of women there has arisen no one greater than John the Baptist. Yet the one who is least in the kingdom of heaven is greater than he."
> - Matthew 11:11

So what will "Heaven" be like?

As we have seen, for both Jesus and John the Baptist, baptism-by-Spirit was a brand-new phenomenon. As such, currently, Heaven was extremely underpopulated. Apart from God and angels, there would only be a handful of the most revered and special Israelite souls:

> "I tell you, many will come from east and west and recline at table with Abraham, Isaac, and Jacob in the kingdom of heaven..."
> - Matthew 8:11

However, this was going to rapidly change: Heaven was going to have an expanding population of baptized-by-spirit Israelite souls. Jesus believed this community would be modeled on an idealized Israel: it would be organized into twelve tribes and there would be a hierarchy but it would be a hierarchy of spiritual merit. The earliest of baptized-by-Spirit souls (i.e., Jesus's disciples) would have authority positions and there would be a king-like figure ("the Son of Man") on a throne.

> Jesus said to them, "Truly, I say to you, in the regeneration[31], when the Son of Man will sit on his

---

[31] Sometimes rendered as "new world" though "regeneration" is apparently closer to the Greek.

glorious throne, you who have followed me will also sit on twelve thrones, judging the twelve tribes of Israel. And everyone who has left houses or brothers or sisters or father or mother or children or lands, for my name's sake, will receive a hundredfold and will inherit eternal life. But many who are first will be last, and the last first."
                                        - Matthew 19:28-30

"You are those who have stayed with me in my trials, and I assign to you, as my Father assigned to me, a kingdom, that you may eat and drink at my table in my kingdom and sit on thrones judging the twelve tribes of Israel."
                                        - Luke 22:28-30

The disciples bought into this hierarchical vision of heaven and there was even lobbying for top positions in heaven:

Then the mother of the sons of Zebedee came up to him with her sons, and kneeling before him she asked him for something. And he said to her, "What do you want?" She said to him, "Say that these two sons of mine are to sit, one at your right hand and one at your left, in your kingdom." Jesus answered, "You do not know what you are asking. Are you able to drink the cup that I am to drink?" They said to him, "We are able." He said to them, "You will drink my cup, but to sit at my right hand and at my left is not mine to grant, but it is for those for whom it has been prepared by my Father." And when the ten heard it, they were indignant at the two brothers. But Jesus called them to him and said, "You know that the rulers of the Gentiles lord it over them, and their great

ones exercise authority over them. It shall not be so among you. But whoever would be great among you must be your servant, and whoever would be first among you must be your slave, even as the Son of Man came not to be served but to serve, and to give his life as a ransom for many."
- Matthew 20

What would the souls do in heaven? Well, there would be at least some earthly pleasures.

"I tell you I will not drink again of this fruit of the vine until that day when I drink it new with you in my Father's kingdom."
- Matthew 26:29

So much for baptized-by-Spirit souls in heaven.

But what of other souls? What of the truly evil souls? The irredeemably hopeless ones? We've already seen that both Jesus and John the Baptist believed that such souls were going to be extinguished in the spiritual equivalent of fire:

"Every tree that does not bear good fruit is cut down and thrown into the fire."
- Matthew 7:19

So what about the in-between souls? The souls that were not evil but have not yet gotten to baptism by the Holy Spirit? The souls that show some promise? As we've seen, they are not going to be thrown into the fiery furnace but are going to be given some time to get their act together (See Luke 13:6-9) But what if these promising souls die? Perhaps they'll spend some time in hell to pay for any sins:

And if your hand causes you to sin, cut it off. It is better for you to enter life crippled than with two hands to go to hell, to the unquenchable fire. And

> if your foot causes you to sin, cut it off. It is better
> for you to enter life lame than with two feet to be
> thrown into hell. And if your eye causes you to
> sin, tear it out. It is better for you to enter the
> kingdom of God with one eye than with two eyes
> to be thrown into hell...
>
> - Mark 9:43-47

And after these not-totally-hopeless souls have purged their bad karma in hell? It seems that Jesus never gives any clear indication about what happens to such souls. As we've seen, some Jews believed in reincarnation so it is possible that Jesus thought that, after paying for their sins in hell, they would be given another chance at incarnation to get to baptism by the Holy Spirit.

Overview of the Parables

The central thesis of this book is that Jesus was a mystic and that "the kingdom of God" is what the soul enters into through "baptism by the Holy Spirit" – what other mystics have referred to as "Union with the One" or "Divine Marriage" or "Union with the Lord of Love".

I believe that I can now lay claim that this thesis has been proven. A telling part of the proof is that it makes sense of the Beatitudes and the Lord's Prayer, and makes sense of parables which previously made no sense – for instance, the parable of the yeast.

Nevertheless, it occurs to me that some readers may be thinking: "Oh, this guy has just cherry-picked the parables that seem to support his case and deliberately ignored the ones that don't."

Accordingly, I am going to briefly reference *all* Jesus's parables in the first three Gospels and how every one of them can be made sense of under the mystic interpretation of the kingdom of God. (There are no parables in the Gospel of John.) I have organized the parables under the broad points they are making. Of course, some parables make more than one point.

1. **God expects to reap fruit from the journey of the souls whether this seems fair or not:**
   - Parable of the Talents (Matt 25:14-30)
   - Ten servants given minas (Luke 19:12-27)

2. **Each soul has an equal chance to experience baptism by the Holy Spirit and so enter the kingdom of God. It doesn't matter how many sins you've committed in the past, where you are in the social order, how prodigal or lost you've been, God still wants you to transform your soul and so be reunited with you:**
   - The Prodigal Son (Luke 15:11-32)
   - Lost sheep (Matt 18:12-14; Luke 15:4-7)
   - Two sons, one obeys, one does not (Matt 21:28-32)
   - Friend in need (Luke 11:5-8)
   - Invitation to a great banquet (Luke 14:16-24)
   - Lost coin (Luke 15:8-10)
   - Moneylender forgives unequal debts (Luke 7:41-43)
   - Workers in the vineyard, early and late (Matt 20:1-16)

3. **The kingdom of God currently within your soul (the spark of the Holy Spirit) is tiny and hidden but it is a pearl beyond price and can grow and transform until there is a fully "grown" soul that is worthy of a "harvest" by God:**
   - Pearl hidden in a field (Matt 13:45-46)
   - Hidden treasure (Matt 13:44)
   - Owner of a house who brings out hidden treasure (Matt 13:52)
   - Mustard seed (Mark 4:30-32)

- Yeast (Matt 13:33; Luke 13:20-21)
- Salt (Matt 5:13). Like yeast, salt is can be spread throughout food while being unseen. If you realize the kingdom of God, your soul will be flavored with the Holy Spirit. Without this, the soul has no zing.
- Growing seed (Mark 4:26-29)

4. **You have to be humble or you will not experience baptism by the Holy Spirit ("Blessed are the meek"):**
   - The Lowest Seat at the feast (Luke 14:7-14)
   - The Master and his Servant (Luke 17:7-10)
   - The Pharisee and the tax collector (Luke 18:10-14)

5. **You have to have mercy (compassion, forgiveness and purity of intent) towards everyone or you will not experience baptism by the Holy Spirit and so enter the kingdom of God ('Blessed are the merciful'):**
   - The Good Samaritan (Luke 10:30-37)
   - The rich man and Lazarus (Luke 16:19-31)
   - The unmerciful servant (Matt 18:23-34)
   - The shrewd manager (Luke 16:1-8) People concerned with things of this world will be dishonest and value dishonesty as a way to getting ahead. People of light have to be above this and be honest in all things big and small.

6. **For baptism by the Holy Spirit to take place, the soul and Spirit have to match. The soul has to be prepared, properly "clothed":**
   - New wine in old wineskins (Mark 2:22; Matt 9:17; Luke 5:37-38)
   - New cloth on an old coat (Mark 2:21; Matt 9:16; Luke 5:36)

- Wedding banquet (Matt 22:2-14). In this parable, the wedding guests have to be clothed correctly for the marriage.

7. **You cannot force the final step of union of the soul with Spirit; you just have to commit, persist, endure, be patient, have depth. You have to deeply hunger and thirst and persist:**
   - The parable of the sower (Mark 4:10-20).
   - Servants must remain watchful (Mark 13:35-37; Luke 12:35-40)
   - Wise and foolish servants (Matt 24:45-51; Luke 12:42-48)
   - Wise and foolish virgins (Matt 25:1-13)
   - Persistent widow and crooked judge (Luke 18:2-8)
   - Cost of discipleship (Luke 14:28-33)

8. **Unfruitful souls who do not experience baptism by the Holy Spirit – or show some promise that they are capable of heading in that direction – are going to be cut down:**
   - Unfruitful fig tree (Luke 13:6-9)
   - Separating weeds from wheat (Matt 13:24-30, 36-43)
   - Separating out bad fish from good (Matt 13:47-50)
   - Separating sheep from goats (Matt 25:31-46)
   - Wicked tenants to be culled (Mark 12:1-11; Matt 21:33-44; Luke 20:9-18)
   - Wedding banquet (Matt 22:2-14). You need to be properly prepared and clothed for the divine marriage or you will be culled.
   - Salt of the earth (Matt 5:13). If your soul does not become properly infused with the salt of spirit, you will be trampled down.

9. **The only secure wealth in life is inner wealth – the transformation of the soul:**
   - Wise and foolish builders (Matt 7:24-27; Luke 6:47-49)
   - Rich man foolishly builds bigger barns (Luke 12:16-21)

10. **Once you have transformed, you need to be prepared to be a beacon for others:**
    - Light of the world (Matt 5:14-15)
    - Lamp on a stand (Mark 4:21-22; Luke 8:16, 11:33)

These are the same parables that Reza Aslan, in his book *Zealot*, described as "abstruse and enigmatic parables that are nearly impossible to understand" (p. 141).

Not anymore.

The black hole

This book has offered you a level of clarity around the teachings of Jesus that you have never come close to before. But there is one black hole that this book has not penetrated and no-one can penetrate. It is the black hole that mystics commonly leave behind: *What actual techniques were being used to purify and transform souls?*

What techniques did John the Baptist use?

No-one knows.

Was it all just prayer? Meditation? If those were the only techniques being used, why keep them secret? Why not spread them around to everyone?

There are at least four reasons why mystics have tended not to publicize their techniques:

1. You have to have a deep hunger and thirst. This isn't a path for dilettantes.
2. The path isn't for everybody. You have to be a strong, mentally stable person to do it. If you're mentally unbalanced, it is not for you.
3. It is generally considered that students need a guide.
4. Concern that the techniques would be seen as social or religious heresy.

What, for instance, if the techniques involved tantric sex? Jesus had both female and male disciples. You could imagine how that would have gone down in 1st Century Palestine.

What if they involved special breathing techniques that could not be evidenced as endorsed by Jewish scripture? John the Baptist's ministry emphasized immersion in water. In the very earliest days of its development in the Twentieth Century, rebirthing/breathwork was done in water. In the 14th Century, St Gregory of Palamas recommended breathing techniques as part of spiritual development (*The Triads*, C I ii 7). Was John doing breathwork in water??

Or was it just prayer and meditation?

It is a black hole. We simply do not know.

The endpoint of the quest for the historical Jesus

We have arrived then at the endpoint of the quest to understand the teachings of the historical Jesus.

He was not a political revolutionary – as Reimarus and, more recently, Reza Aslan argued.

He was not, first and foremost, a preacher of a forthcoming apocalypse – as has been the received academic view of Jesus for over a century.

Jesus was primarily what most people have always suspected he was – a spiritual teacher. But he was not teaching "Act *good, believe in me, and go to heaven*". He was teaching the mystic path of inner spiritual evolution: an evolution of your soul that can only happen while you are incarnate in a human body. It cannot happen after you die.

Jesus, like his teacher John, believed that this signified that the Old Covenant of Moses had been superseded. Israelites could no longer coast along, thinking that being born an Israelite and obeying Mosaic Law was going to do the job. People had to set themselves on the path of inner transformation or else they would be caught up in a reckoning of souls. God would separate the wheat from the chaff (Matt 3:12), the sheep from the goats (Matt 25:32-33), the souls with promise from the hopeless souls. And the latter would be annihilated.

Why?

Why did John and Jesus believe in a forthcoming reckoning of souls?

It is not typical of mystics. There is nothing apocalyptic in *The Upanishads*. Nor in Meister Eckhart. Not in St Teresa of Avila. Nor in Plotinus. And they all went through union of the soul with spirit.

Why did these two particular Israelite mystics think that what they were experiencing indicated a reckoning of souls was on its way? Was there something different about their experiences? Remember these questions... They will be answered in *The Crucifixion Code.*

Part VI

Jesus Now

"But who do you say that I am?"

- Mark 8:29

The two Jesus's

There are two Jesus's.

There is the Jesus of faith. He was the only begotten Son of God. He was born from a virgin. His birth was foretold and heralded by angels. He never did any inner spiritual work because he never had to. He was born perfect. He was born with huge spiritual knowledge such that he could lecture priests at the age of twelve. He was born to preach the kingdom of God on behalf of his heavenly Father. For some unknowable reason, he decided to twiddle his thumbs and not actually start on this mission until around his 30th year. John the Baptist only existed as a butler to announce his arrival. The descent of the Holy Spirit at the River Jordan was just a tick of approval from God. The Transfiguration – well, that didn't have a purpose at all.

Such is the Jesus of faith.

It's ludicrous. It's incoherent. And it is out of alignment with the most reliable parts of the Gospels.

And then there is Yeshua, the real historical Jesus. This is what this book has pursued. In a Zen-like paradox, this book has been about demystifying Jesus so that we can see him as the flesh-and-blood mystic he was.

Of course, the vast majority of academic historians can only come so far along this journey. I have presented overwhelming evidence that Jesus talked like a mystic, thought like a mystic, believed that the soul could be transformed and baptized by Spirit. But your average historian will likely leap off the bus when it comes to admitting that such spiritual transformations actually happen. Yet we have seen masses of intersubjective evidence that this is the case: mystics from across disparate ages and cultures and languages attesting to the same experience.

Why believe that Jesus was a mystic preaching the mystic path? Why not persist with the received academic idea that Jesus was just a deluded apocalyptic prophet? Why not go with the idea that the "kingdom of God" refers to the overthrow of Roman occupation and establishing a theocratic new state of Israel?

There are three over-arching reasons. They involve the same criteria we apply when assessing scientific theories:

1. Internal consistency;
2. Intersubjective attestation;
3. Explanatory Power.

Internal Consistency

The picture which this book paints of Jesus's life and teachings is internally consistent. It contains no self-contradictions – unlike the common Christian faith which requires Jesus to be both fully God and fully man.

Intersubjective attestation

Science is an empirical discipline – i.e., it is ultimately underpinned by what are called "intersubjective experiences". These are experiences which virtually everyone has under the same condition. Thus, a scientific theory may be inspired by a dream (as was Kekulé's uncovering of the molecular structure of benzene) but the evidence for it has to be experiences that pretty much anyone could have.

In an identical manner, what has been evidenced in this book is the commonality of experiences by mystics across the ages. The experience of union of the soul with Spirit is intersubjective. Anyone who goes through the same processes will eventually experience the same thing. The parallels between what Jesus said and what is written by other mystics are just too close. They are overwhelming intersubjective evidence that Jesus was a mystic.

Explanatory Power

The mystic interpretation of Jesus's ministry explains far, far, far more about what Jesus said than any other theory. It makes sense of the parables which otherwise do not make sense – the parable of the mustard seed, the parable of the yeast, the parable of the ten virgins... It actually explains each and every one of the parables. It makes sense of the Beatitudes. It explains Jesus's use of the terms "kingdom of God" and "the Holy Spirit". It makes sense of the Lord's Prayer. No other theory comes anywhere near as close to explaining so much of the recorded words of Jesus.

The return to realizing the kingdom of God

This book has given you the chance to understand the teachings of the most impactful person in the history of this planet. Perhaps you struggled to wrap your brain around it. You may have to go back to the beginning of this book and read it again.

Over and above this, you have been given a chance to arrive at a truer understanding of not just Jesus but of yourself – of the spiritual realities that lie under the chatter of your mind.

> "Do not lay up for yourselves treasures on earth, where moth and rust destroy and where thieves break in and steal, but lay up for yourselves treasures in heaven, where neither moth nor rust destroys and where thieves do not break in and steal."
>
> - Matthew 6:19-20

This is what the message of Jesus and John the Baptist offered then and offers now: the chance to lay up treasures within... treasures that the earthly world cannot touch... the treasure of an evolved soul... the permanent transformation of a baptized-by-spirit soul... to experience the descent of the Holy Spirit... to fuse your soul with the great spiritual field... to become involved in the evolution of the spiritual universe.

But first, you must be poor in spirit and mourn. Without a haunted sense of a void in your life – an ache for true meaningfulness – you'll never start on the inner path. *There has to be more to life than this.*

Second, you must be meek. You have to be humble. Vanity will surely block the path. *I don't have all the answers after all. Maybe somebody else does.*

Third, you must be hungry. You must deeply hunger and thirst to be right on the inside. *Something inside me has to change. The external world is not going to do it for me.*

Fourth, you must embrace mercifulness – forgiveness, compassion, purity of intent.

Fifth, you must start to work on the purification of your soul. This will bring on visions.

Sixth, the further purification of your soul – turning traumatized energies into the pure energies of Peace, Love, Beingness...

Seventh, baptism by the Holy Spirit – fusion of the soul with Spirit.

This is the path.

It is the one true spiritual path.

It is the path which Jesus preached.

Only treading this path will give you experiences that irrevocably confirm the writings in this book.

It is way past time for Christianity to abandon the artificial construct of the Kingdom of Jesus and get back to what Jesus actually taught: the union of the soul with the Holy Spirit, inner spiritual evolution.

Great Christian thinkers and writers such as St Augustine, St Francis and Thomas à Kempis believed that there is only one true Christian way: to imitate Christ. This book has shown that the imitation of Jesus means following the path of the Beatitudes, the path of inner transformation.

When you close this book, what then? Will you become the fertile soil? Or will you be hardened rock that this knowledge bounces off?

> Jesus said, "I took my stand in the midst of the world, and in flesh I appeared to them. I found them all drunk, and I did not find any of them thirsty. My soul ached for the children of humanity because they are blind in their hearts and do not see, for they came into the world empty, and they also seek to depart from the world empty. But meanwhile they are drunk. When they shake off their wine, then they will change their ways."
>
> - Gospel of Thomas 28

What is it that you are drunk on?

Are you drunk on the pride of how much you know?

Are you drunk on games?

On alcohol?

Drugs?

On your career?

Your family?

On love?

Are you drunk on your religious faith?

Are you drunk on atheism and the pride that your "superior knowledge" gives you?

Underneath that drunkenness... muffled by that drunkenness... there is a voice crying out in the inner wilderness.... *There has to be more to life than this.*

> An ass which turns a millstone did a hundred miles walking. When it was loosed, it found that it was still at the same place.
> - Gospel of Philip 56

Don't let this be your life.

*****

Complete Your Understanding of Jesus

The Crucifixion Code

After 2,000 years...
The truth...

The truth about why Jesus was crucified.
The truth about why it became the most
impactful event in human history.

Ren Lexander

Part of *The Meaning of Life* series

A series of dramatic events is about to come in rapid-fire succession:

1. The execution of John the Baptist
2. The announcement by Jesus that he would head to Jerusalem to suffer and die – and so he abruptly abandons his mission of preaching the kingdom of God.
3. The first mention by Jesus of a forthcoming apocalyptic reckoning of souls to be led by "the Son of Man".
4. Transfiguration
5. Jerusalem: Arrest, torture, crucifixion.

The natural conclusion is that, somehow, all these things are linked... but how?

You will learn:

- Why Jesus suddenly abandoned his mission of preaching the kingdom of God and instead set his face towards Jerusalem and crucifixion.
- What "Transfiguration" is.
- Why Jesus started talking to his disciples about a forthcoming apocalypse.
- Who "the Son of Man" was.
- The truth about the "betrayal" by Judas
- Why Jesus's crucifixion became the most impactful event in human history
- And much more...

Check out/buy The Crucifixion Code at Amazon.com:

Appendices

Spiritual research will give the Gospels back to mankind.

> - Rudolf Steiner, *The Christ Impulse and the development of ego consciousness*

The Wilderness: Jesus's time with John

The wilderness, the opening section of Part I, is a colorized version of the black-and-white accounts found in the first three Gospels (Mark 1:1-15; Luke 3:1-22; Matt 3-4).

The Gospel of Luke comments on Jesus's age: "Jesus, when he began his ministry, was about thirty years of age..." (3:23)

All four Biblical Gospels agree that Jesus did not start his ministry until after meeting with John the Baptist.

The four Gospels were originally penned in Greek, and the Greek word for Jesus's prior occupation is "*tekton*" which has been traditionally translated as "carpenter" (Mark 6:3).[32] We have to lose the modern image of carpenters as being well-to-do tradesmen driving around in air-conditioned vans with expensive power tools. It seems likely that Jesus would have not been living in tiny Nazareth as there would have been little work. Reza Aslan in *Zealot* mounts a sensible case that Jesus likely pursued work in the nearby bustling city of Sepphoris.

The Gospel of Mark, the earliest and most reliable of the Gospels, starts not with the over-the-top nativity stories but with Jesus going out into the wilderness where he is baptized by John. John the Baptist is the first person in the New Testament to talk about the "Holy Spirit", baptism by the Holy Spirit (Mark 1:8), and "the

---

[32] I do not read Greek so I am dependent on others for translations and discussions of translations. I note that no translation of the Gospels has ever been done by someone empathetic to the idea that Jesus was a mystic. Perhaps this book will be the spark that provokes a Greek scholar to do such a translation.

kingdom of God" – or, as it is generally rendered in the Gospel of Matthew, "the kingdom of heaven".

> John appeared, baptizing in the wilderness preaching a baptism of repentance...
> - Mark 1:4.

> In those days John the Baptist appeared in the wilderness of Judea, proclaiming, "Repent, for the kingdom of heaven is at hand."
> - Matthew 3:1-2

The English word "repent" has come to be associated with repentance of sin. So we now tend to automatically read such passages as "repent your sins for the kingdom of heaven is at hand". This sounds threatening – like, if you don't repent your sins, God is coming to get you. The Greek word traditionally translated as "repent" is μετάνοια (metanoia). This is a compound of "*meta*" (after, beyond, above) and the verb "*noeo*" (to think or perceive). So *metanoia* could be translated as: "to think differently after" or "to think beyond". *Metanoia* is a re-thinking, a reflection accompanied by a change of heart, mind or consciousness. The Greek word has no sense of looking back in regret. Arguably few translations in history have been more disastrous in their effects than the translation of *metanoia* as "repent". It has been described as "a linguistic and theological tragedy"[33]. In *The Complete Gospels*, the translating scholars render *metanoia* as "change of heart" (Mark 1:4) and "change your ways" (Matt 3:1).

---

[33] A. T. Robertson, Word Pictures in the New Testament – 2 Corinthians, p. 29. Available free online at:
http://www.ccel.org/ccel/robertson_at/wp_2cor.pdf.
For more, see the article "Metanoia" at Wikipedia.

The association of *metanoia* with "going beyond" or "thinking beyond" is fascinating in light of John the Baptist and Jesus teaching that Jews had to now go beyond the old covenant of Moses. (See discussion of this in "Did Matthew understand the Beatitudes" in Part III, and "The Death of the Old Covenant" and "The New Covenant" in Part V.)

However, I think a more appropriately modern translation of *metanoia* is what we now may say to people who are going around in a daze and not fully aware of what they should be aware of: "Wake up!"

See Luke 3:7-14 for a dialogue between John the Baptist and the crowd he was preaching to.

It is recorded that Jesus stayed in the wilderness for 40 days (Mark 1:13). Numbers in the Bible are used symbolically not arithmetically. Forty is, symbolically, the number of completion. Jesus stayed in the wilderness long enough to complete. No-one has the vaguest idea about how long he stayed there in calendar time. It could have been many months. It could have been years. Considering he did enough inner spiritual work to experience baptism by the Holy Spirit, he was probably there for a year... or two... or more?

The writer of Mark couldn't get around the conjoined facts that Jesus went out to the wilderness to be baptized by John and then stayed out there a long time. To get around the obvious conclusion that he spent this time under the guidance of John, Jesus's time with John the Baptist is absurdly reduced to minutes and the rest of the time he just spends wandering around the wilderness.

The Gospel of Mark (1:13) records Jesus as having been tempted in the wilderness. The ultimate temptation would have been to leave the wilderness and return to the normal world before he had completed his spiritual journey with John. It is likely that Jesus talked about this temptation with his disciples and that this got mythically translated into being tempted by Satan (Mark 1:13).

See Part III for a discussion of visions and feelings of peace along the spiritual path.

Generally the Holy Spirit is portrayed as descending like a dove. Apparently, the literal translation of the Greek in Mark 1:10 is "enter into" rather than "descend" as it has been traditionally translated.

Luke 3:21-22 records the baptism by the Holy Spirit as not happening during the baptism in the River Jordan but sometime after that and during a spiritual practice: "...and when Jesus also had been baptized and was praying, the heaven opened, and the Holy Spirit descended upon him in bodily form like a dove." (See Appendix Two for a discussion of the Gospel of Luke.)

After this entry of the Holy Spirit, "a voice came from heaven" (Mark 1:11). Faith-based Christians tend to read this as if it was a miraculous voice external to Jesus manifesting out of thin air but this isn't what's portrayed in the Gospel of Mark. If it was an external event, John the Baptist and the others there would have reacted to this miraculous voice.

The oldest known version of the Gospel of Luke records this spiritual voice as saying: "You are my son; today I have become your Father." (Luke 3:22). Scribes would later alter the passage to make it more in line with the doctrine in which they believed – i.e., that Jesus was already the Son of God. So what you will now find in most Bibles is the doctored version: "You are my Son, the Beloved; with you I am well pleased." You will find a translation of the original, undoctored version in Robert J. Miller (ed), *The Complete Gospels*. For a discussion of this verse, see Bart D. Ehrman, *Misquoting Jesus*, pp. 158-161. It should be noted that the writer of the Gospel of Luke

186

had access to an earlier version of the Gospel of Mark than we do. It may well be that Luke reproduced the original version of Mark.

> Yeshua revealed [beside the] Jordan the fullness of the Kingdom of Heaven, which existed before the totality. Moreover he was begotten as Son, moreover he was anointed, moreover he was atoned...[34]

Despite this profound inner transformation, Jesus does not start his ministry until after John the Baptist is arrested (Mark 1:14; Matthew 4:12-17). There has to be a reason for this. It is possible that John forbade his students to preach – possibly to protect them from the dangers of so doing. It seems likely that John took his star pupils aside and asked them to start preaching should anything happen to him. John likely told Jesus that he had to be prepared to act as a light for others – just as Jesus would later tell his students (Matt 5:14-15; Mark 4:21-22).

In the early days of his mission, Jesus says: "I must preach the good news of the kingdom of God to the other towns as well; for I was sent for this purpose" (Luke 4:43.). The logical thing to conclude is that this "sending" came from his teacher, John the Baptist. The most likely reason for sending Jesus into the towns is that John had other students who, like Jesus, had experienced baptism by the Holy Spirit, and John had already assigned them to take over the mission by the River Jordan and preach in cities such as Jerusalem and Sepphoris. Accordingly, John assigned Jesus the mission of taking the word out to villages and towns. This would explain why,

---

[34] This passage is from the remarkable Gospel of Philip (88). I have changed the phrase "Sovereignty of Heaven" to "Kingdom of Heaven" which is the phrase used in the Isenberg translation – noting that this has been translated from Coptic not Greek. See the discussion of the Gospel of Philip in Appendix Two.

after John's arrest, Jesus did not take over John's ministry by the River Jordan; and why he never preached in major cities like Sepphoris even though he preached near there; and why he never preached in Jerusalem until he went there in the last few days of his life – and even then, in the Gospels of Luke and Mark, he never mentions the kingdom of God! Likely Jerusalem and those areas were assigned to other students of John. Moreover, when John the Baptist is languishing in prison, he sends out a question to Jesus: "Are you the one who is to be next or should we look for another?" (Matt 11:3). This strongly indicates that there were other candidates out there, other students of John who were carrying on John's ministry in other places.

I have intimated that the chief priests might have influenced Herod's decision to arrest John the Baptist. This possibility is not raised in the Bible. Given the power of the priesthood and John the Baptist's fame as a spiritual preacher, it seems unlikely that Herod would have proceeded against John without at least checking with the senior priesthood. It is more likely still that the senior priests had a proactive involvement. We know that the attitude of the high priests to Jesus was toxic to the point of lethal. Why would their attitude have been any different to John the Baptist who was preaching the same things?

This may account for Jesus's global dislike of Pharisees and priests – he thought they colluded in the arrest of John. "Woe to you, scribes and Pharisees, hypocrites! For you build the tombs of the prophets and decorate the graves of the righteous..." (Matthew 23:29)

Collusions are referred to several times in the Gospel of Mark. Early on in his ministry, Jesus upsets the Pharisees and the "Pharisees went out and immediately conspired with the Herodians against him, how to destroy him." (Mark 3:6) Most likely "Herodians" were a religious sect with a particular affiliation and loyalty to the Herod family. Note that King Herod directed the appointments of High Priests.

As Jesus's ministry progresses, the Pharisees demand a sign which Jesus doesn't give to them. Jesus warns the disciples against trusting the Pharisees and the Herodians: they are poisonous. "Watch out! Beware of the yeast of the Pharisees and the yeast of Herodians!" (Mark 8:15; ISV) [35] Later, when Jesus is in Jerusalem, the chief priests "sent to him some of the Pharisees and some of the Herodians, to trap him in his talk." (Mark 12:13).

We know that the chief priests lied to Pontius Pilate in order to get Jesus crucified – saying that Jesus promoted himself as "King of the Jews" – words that never came out of Jesus's mouth. These same priests certainly would not have hesitated to embellish the words of John the Baptist in order to poison Herod's mind against him and cause him to arrest John.

One can well imagine a scenario like this.... The high priests decide that they want to get rid of John the Baptist. They send out some lap-dog Pharisees to question John (as they later did with Jesus) and they try to trip him up. The Pharisees ask John: "What do you say about Herod's marriage to Herodias, the wife of his brother?" John would cite that, under Jewish Law, it was wrong. The high priests then use the Herodians to get word to Herod that John the Baptist is polemically denouncing Herod and his foul marriage. This brings on the arrest of John and ultimately his death.

Prior to Jesus's arrest in Jerusalem, Jesus has only one direct conversation with the chief priests. On all other occasions, they sent minions to do their work – Pharisees and Sadducees. But this

---

[35] Some ancient authorities read "the yeast of Herod' but obviously "Herodians" makes much more sense.

one time they cross paths as Jesus is walking in the temple. "As he was walking in the temple, the chief priests, the scribes and the elders came to him." (Mark 11:27) What is it that they ask Jesus at this sole encounter? They want to know by what authority this upstart country bumpkin preacher presumes to think he has a greater spiritual truth than they do. "By what authority are you doing these things, or who gave you this authority to do them?" (Mark 11:28) Jesus looks at these men. He has no need to answer them at all. Or he could have just said: "*My words speak for themselves. Either they are true or they are not.*" But instead, he looks them in the eye and raises the ghost of John the Baptist. Jesus said to them, "I will ask you one question; answer me, and I will tell you by what authority I do these things. Was the baptism of John from heaven or from man? Answer me." (Mark 11:29-30)

But these priests and scribes aren't game to jump one way or the other. "We do not know."

Jesus answers them disdainfully. "Neither will I tell you by what authority I do these things." (Mark 11:33)

The role of the high priests in John's arrest and demise is not recounted in the Bible but it certainly makes sense. Plus it explains exactly why Jesus had such disdain for the Pharisees and the Herodians and the senior priests.

Sources

Hereinafter follow comments on the sources which I have drawn upon. If you wish to know more about particular sources, I would suggest you start by checking out the relevant entry in Wikipedia. If you want more depth after that, I recommend the well-written books of Bart D. Ehrman (see Bibliography).

Historicity

When it comes to understanding the historical Jesus, we are not blessed with written accounts from the man himself nor even writings which can be reliably attributed to eyewitnesses. Instead there were oral traditions which, years or decades after the death of Jesus, were written down in Greek. Jesus himself would have spoken Aramaic.

As in all historical assessments, there is a rule of thumb that, all other things being equal, earlier sources are better sources. For instance, the Gospel of Mark was written decades before the Gospel of John. This in itself lends the Gospel of Mark a greater measure of credence as a record of the life and words of the historical Jesus.

When New Testament scholars seek to evaluate the historical reliability of a passage about Jesus, they use three main criteria:

1. The criterion of independent attestation.

Does the event appear independently in more than one source? If it does, then this gives it more weight to be considered to be historically accurate – just as, at a modern-day legal trial, several eyewitnesses independently agreeing in their accounts is more compelling than one.

The following sources are considered to be independent:

- The Gospel of Mark
- The Gospel of John
- The Gospel of Thomas
- "Q"
- "L"
- "M"
- The letters of Paul

(See below for discussion of these sources.)

If all or almost all of these independently refer to some event then this gives independent attestation of the event. This is true, for instance, both of the crucifixion and Jesus going out to be baptized by John the Baptist which are referenced in all sources. Of course, it is perfectly possible that some event may have happened but only have been attested to in one source. Nevertheless, independent attestation does lend greater weight to its likelihood.

2. The criterion of dissimilarity

Is this something that a true believer in Jesus would be likely to make up or is it **dissimilar** to something that a true believer would want in there but, nevertheless, it IS in there?

For instance, in the Gospel of Matthew 11:11, Jesus says, "Truly, I say to you, among those born of women there has arisen no one greater than John the Baptist." This is Jesus placing John the Baptist equal to or above himself and so it is extraordinarily dissimilar to what a faith-based Gospel-writer would invent.

This gives this passage significant brownie points to be considered as historically accurate.

3. The criterion of contextual credibility

Is this something that would have or could have happened in first-century Palestine?

This criterion arguably counts against significant slabs of the Gospel of John. How Jesus talks in this Gospel just does not ring true to how a country preacher in 1st Century Palestine would talk. By contrast, how Jesus talks in the Gospel of Mark has significantly more contextual credibility.

One example of contextual credibility is the appearance of Aramaic phrases. The Gospels were originally written in Greek but Jesus would have spoken Aramaic. The multiple appearances of Aramaic phrases in the Gospel of Mark lend contextual credibility.

Biblical Sources

Jesus spoke Aramaic but, apart from a handful of Aramaic phrases, the Biblical Gospels were written in Greek because, back then, Greek was the "lingua Franca" of the Mediterranean. Greek was the equivalent to what English is today. Even the Hebrew Bible (i.e., the "Old Testament") was then mainly being read in Greek and not Hebrew. Greek was widespread because of the conquests by Alexander the Great and his vision of uniting nations into one world.

The attribution of a particular Gospel to a particular disciple such as "Mark" or "Matthew" is, let us say, "honorific". We don't know for certain who wrote them.

The first three Gospels – Mark, Matthew and Luke – are referred to as the "Synoptic Gospels" because they are, largely, in sync and can be "seen together" (syn-optic). By contrast, the Gospel of John is wildly different.

In places, the Gospels contradict each other. A few of many examples:

- The Gospel of Mark has Jesus crucified on the day of the Passover; the Gospel of John has him crucified on the day before the Passover.
- In the Gospels of Mark and Matthew, Jesus does not start preaching until after the arrest of John the Baptist. In the Gospel of John, Jesus is preaching prior to John the Baptist's arrest.
- The Gospel of Luke and the Gospel of Matthew both have nativity accounts but they are almost entirely different. In Matthew, after the birth, Joseph and Mary flee to Egypt. In Luke, they return to Nazareth. What most people think of as Jesus's nativity is an amalgam of the two.
- The Gospels of Luke and Matthew both list Jesus's family tree but they are radically different.

I do not read Greek so I have been dependent on translations by others and reading discussions of alternative translations. I have generally used the translation of the English Standard Version except where specified. The other translations I draw on are the International Standard Version (ISV), the New International Version (NIV), English Revised Edition (ERE), the King James Version (KJV), and R.J. Miller (ed), *The Complete Gospels*. I have no compunction about picking and choosing between different translations as there is no such thing as a definitive translation. Moreover, this book has been executed at a huge disadvantage. Many translations of the Gospels have been slanted by the translator's belief that Jesus was the only begotten son of God for all eternity. At the other end of the spectrum, the translations in R.J. Miller (ed), *The Complete Gospels*, are slanted by an assumption of the correctness of the academic view of Jesus – that he was a failed apocalyptic preacher. See *The Complete Gospels*, p. 12, where it is admitted that their translation of "*Basileia tou Theo*" (the kingdom of God) was rendered as "God's imperial rule" to fit in with an apocalyptic view of Jesus's teachings.

There has *never* been a translation of the Gospels empathetic to the ideas in this book – that Jesus was a mystic teaching the path of inner transformation. One of my hopes is that, in the wake of this book, a Greek scholar will do such a translation. It would be more than intriguing to see what emerges.

I have generally rendered the Greek word "Christos" into its Jewish form of "Messiah" as this gives it a more valid historical flavor.

www.biblehub.com is a great resource for comparing translations.

The Dating of the Biblical Gospels

Christianity was initially spread by word of mouth – not surprising in a world where something like 97% of the world was illiterate.

Compounding this, one of the primary spreaders of the Jesus movement was the Apostle Paul who preached that a Second Coming of Jesus was going to happen any day now. As such, the point of writing stuff down for one's children and one's children's children – not that great. Paul never met the living Jesus or heard him speak so he was not well equipped to spread the actual teachings of Jesus.

Sooner or later, a few key individuals started writing the oral tradition down.

There is a very broad consensus that the Gospel of John was the last Gospel written, probably somewhere around the end of the first Century. The Jesus in this Gospel is very remote from the earthy parable-preacher of the three Synoptic Gospels.

The Synoptic Gospels are considered by academics to have been written down in this order: Mark, Matthew, Luke. One of the major reasons for this ordering is that both Matthew and Luke draw heavily on the Gospel of Mark. Luke actually admits that he is writing a composite Gospel drawing on previous writings (Luke 1:1-4).

A common academic dating for the Synoptic Gospels is something like this:

- The Gospel of Mark 70 A.D.
- The Gospel of Matthew 80 A.D.
- The Gospel of Luke 80-90 A.D.

This would mean that the first Gospel, Mark, was written down around 40 years after the death of Jesus.

I believe that these datings for the Synoptic Gospels are far too late.

There is actually a Gospel which more-or-less dates itself. This is the Gospel of Luke. The author of this also wrote the Acts of the Apostles. Together they comprise around a quarter of the New Testament. It is a sprawling narrative often referred to by scholars as Luke-Acts. Acts of the Apostles ends with the Apostle Paul living in Rome awaiting trial – a trial which would culminate in his execution. There is no reason why Acts would end at this point unless this was actually the state of affairs at the time the author finished writing. If Paul had already been martyred for his faith, the author would have put it in the Gospel, boasting about how he'd died in the name of Jesus. But he didn't record this. This would date the writing of Acts (and therefore the writing of the Gospel of Luke) at around 61 A.D.

In this case, the Gospel of Mark would have had to have been written before 61 A.D. – possibly decades before that. The academic dating of the Gospel of Mark at 70 A.D. seems to be based on one solitary passage:

> And as he came out of the temple, one of his disciples said to him, "Look, Teacher, what wonderful stones and what wonderful buildings!" And Jesus said to him, "Do you see these great buildings? There will not be left here one stone upon another that will not be thrown down."
> - Mark 13:1-2

The academic reasoning seems to be this: Ah, this was Jesus "predicting" the destruction of the Temple in Jerusalem but this only happened in 70 A.D. when the Romans sacked the city. Therefore, the Gospel of Mark was written after the destruction of the Temple or when this destruction seemed inevitable. So this "prediction" was never said by the historical Jesus but was written into Jesus's mouth by Mark to make it look like Jesus made an accurate prediction.

I absolutely do not understand why this is seen as a "prediction" at all. This is the classic way mystics teach students. Far and away, the most gob-smacking physical thing that the disciples would ever see in their entire lives was the Second Temple in Jerusalem. It was like the Vatican, the Taj Mahal and the Sydney Opera House all rolled up into one. In response to his disciples' awe, Jesus says: "Yes, yes. All very impressive but it is ephemeral. It will all pass." Everything physical passes away. Only things of the spirit endure. The evolution of the soul is the only way to build your house upon a rock that will forever endure (see Matthew 7:24-27).

Moreover, if the author of the Gospel of Mark was writing in 70 A.D. and wanted to put successful predictions into the mouth of Jesus, he could have put a lot more predictions in than just this solitary one. He could have put in predictions involving Jewish rebellion and short-term triumphs and the revenge of Rome. This was no prediction by Jesus. It was simply a mystic teacher pointing out the ephemeral nature of the physical.

On this basis then, the Gospel of Mark could be dated decades earlier than the traditional academic dating; and that means that the Gospels of Matthew and Luke could have also been written decades earlier than the traditional datings.

The Gospel of Mark could have easily been written down in 40 A.D. or even earlier.

We can also draw an illuminating contrast between the Gospel of Mark and the Gospel of John. That later Gospel, written so very many decades after the death of Jesus, eliminated any incident or saying that did not support the idea that Jesus was the Son of God. If the Gospel of Mark was written four decades after the death of Jesus, isn't that also what would have happened? Any discomforting passages in the oral tradition would have been culled? Instead, there are many many things in the Gospel of Mark which are dissimilar to what a Jesus follower would want to hear. Just a few of many, many examples:

- Jesus's mother and brothers thinking he had totally lost the plot by starting to preach (Mark 3:21)
- Jesus being rejected by his hometown (Mark 6:1-6)
- Jesus failing to heal people (Mark 6:5)
- The Transfiguration - which makes no sense for someone who was already the Son of God (Mark 9:2-8)

- Jesus calling out on the Cross: "My God, my God, why hast thou forsaken me?" (Mark 15:34)

- The naked man: this being the most bizarre incident in the entire Gospel of Mark; one that no-one has an explanation for and which was deleted from subsequent Gospels. After Jesus is arrested in the Garden of Gethsemane and as he is being led away for trial, the following incident is recorded: "And a young man followed him, with nothing but a linen cloth about his body. And they seized him, but he left the linen cloth and ran away naked." (Mark 14:51-52)

Given passages which are so dissimilar to what Jesus followers would want to hear or would ever make up, the onus is on the academics who want to date the Synoptic Gospels so late (70 A.D. or later) to make a comprehensively convincing case. They haven't. The case that all three Synoptic Gospels were written before the execution of Paul is stronger.

As such, the Gospel of Mark may have been written only a handful of years after the death of Jesus. A final strong piece of evidence for this is that, despite being written in Greek, the Gospel of Mark features dramatic Aramaic words and phrases. Surely Aramaic phrases would have been one of the things most likely to be eroded away and discarded over time.

The Gospel of Mark

The Gospel of Mark is the earliest of the four Biblical Gospels. It has a very appealing, minimalist, bare-bones feel to it. The Gospel of Mark is virtually universally considered by Biblical scholars to be the earliest and most reliable source for events in Jesus's life. By contrast, The Gospel of Thomas and "Q" (see below) are sayings gospels. They contain few biographical details but have significant credibility as containing things that Jesus said – or being close to what he said.

The Gospel of Mark has no nativity scenes and starts with the figure of John the Baptist.

Scholars agree that the actual Gospel of Mark ended at 16:8. Women go to the tomb of Jesus, find it empty, and a young man sitting there. They run away terrified. Subsequent scenes of disciples talking to a risen Jesus were tacked on the end of the Gospel of Mark by later writers.

There is an identifiable tension in the Gospel of Mark between the author's dedication to getting the details of Jesus's life and teachings accurate on one hand and, on the other hand, making points about Jesus that Jesus-followers believed and wanted to hear. Some examples of this tension:

1. **Jesus was superior to John the Baptist even though Jesus never said so**

   So he puts the words that Jesus was superior into the mouth of John the Baptist (Mark 1:7-8).

2. **Jesus was the Son of God even though he never said so**

   So, amazingly, Mark puts the words claiming that Jesus is the Son of God into the mouths of people possessed by impure spirits (Mark 3:10-12) and a Gentile Roman soldier at Jesus's crucifixion (Mark 15:37-39)!

3. **Jesus was the Jewish Messiah even though he never says so**

   So, instead, the claim that Jesus was the Messiah comes out of the mouth of the disciple Peter (Mark 8:29).

4. Jesus could have risen after three days

Fascinatingly, the author of the Gospel of Mark records no incidents where the risen Jesus is seen; but, as Mark knows that such stories are rife, he has the story of an empty tomb so that at least allows for the possibility of a risen Jesus:

> When the Sabbath was past, Mary Magdalene, Mary the mother of James, and Salome bought spices, so that they might go and anoint him. And very early on the first day of the week, when the sun had risen, they went to the tomb. And they were saying to one another, "Who will roll away the stone for us from the entrance of the tomb?" And looking up, they saw that the stone had been rolled back – it was very large. And entering the tomb, they saw a young man sitting on the right side, dressed in a white robe, and they were alarmed. And he said to them, "Do not be alarmed. You seek Jesus of Nazareth, who was crucified. He has risen; he is not here. See the place where they laid him. But go, tell his disciples and Peter that he is going before you to Galilee. There you will see him, just as he told you." And they went out and fled from the tomb, for trembling and astonishment had seized them, and they said nothing to anyone, for they were afraid.
>
> - Mark 16:1-8

The most puzzling part of this is at the end: "...and they said nothing to anyone, for they were afraid". If they said nothing to anyone, how did anyone else ever find out about it? How did Mark, the author of this Gospel, ever find out about it?

Speculation: Is this Mark making up an excuse for why he'd never heard a story about an empty tomb from a reliable source – but, nevertheless, had to put the story in to allow the possibility of sightings of a resurrected Jesus?

5. The Apocalypse will be very apocalyptic

The Jesus-followers around this time must have been extremely dedicated to the belief in a forthcoming apocalypse because this is the subject where Mark's dedication to capturing the actual words of Jesus seems to be thrown out the window. The Gospel of Mark (13:3-37) has an amazingly long Jesus monologue on a forthcoming apocalypse – a monologue so long that no-one could possibly have recalled it verbatim. This is not to say that Jesus never said anything apocalyptic, but it does seem likely that the author of Mark threw in everything he had and then some into this speech.

*

The Greek in the Gospel of Mark is apparently fairly low-class and was often "enhanced" by the writers of the Gospels of Matthew and Luke. They also took it upon themselves to fill in perceived gaps. This seems to especially be the case with the Gospel of Matthew. The following is one example of Matthew adding to the Gospel of Mark. It occurs just after Jesus informs his disciples that he must suffer and die.

The original Markan version:

> And Peter took him aside and began to rebuke him. But turning and seeing his disciples, he rebuked Peter and said, "Get behind me, Satan!

For you are not setting your mind on the things of God, but on the things of man."

- Mark 8:32-33.

Behold the embellishment in the Gospel of Matthew:

And Peter took him aside and began to rebuke him, saying, "Far be it from you, Lord! This shall never happen to you." But he turned and said to Peter, "Get behind me, Satan! You are a hindrance to me. For you are not setting your mind on the things of God, but on the things of man."

- Matthew 16:22-23

This is pretty obviously an imaginative Matthew fill-in. If Peter took Jesus aside, it would be because he did not want anyone to hear what he was going to say to Jesus. So who heard and recorded this (apart from Peter)? By contrast, bystanders would have heard Jesus's strong reply. The author of the Gospel of Matthew has surely written words into Peter's mouth.

In understanding the relationship of Mark to the other synoptic Gospels of Matthew and Luke, it should be kept in mind that Luke and Matthew had access to much earlier versions of Mark than we do. Because of this, it is possible that some of the passages of the Gospel of Luke or Matthew are more like the original words of Mark than the version of Mark that has survived into the present. This becomes more compelling when Luke and Matthew render a passage of Mark in an identical way, but the passage is rendered differently in Mark. For instance, when Jesus is undergoing a grilling by the high priests, they ask him if he is the Son of the Blessed One. In Mark 14:62, the answer is "I am". In both Matthew and Luke, the equivalent answer is much vaguer. In Matthew, it is "You have said so" (26:64); in Luke, it is "You say that I am." (22:70). It is possible but *highly unlikely* that both Matthew and Luke coincidentally changed the very direct reply in Mark into something vaguer. But they would have no reason to do so. The other alternative is that they accurately rendered the original version of Mark and the version of Mark that we now have been altered to the more absolute: "I am". Certainly, a faith-based Christian scribe would have a vested interest in changing Jesus's reply to the less ambivalent "I am". Or, indeed, there could have been an accidental omission of a few words.

Q (50 AD? Possibly earlier)

"Q" stands for "Quelle" which is German for "source". An independent copy of Q has never been found. It has been reconstructed by extracting out the passages in Luke and Matthew that are virtually identical but not found in the Gospel of Mark. You can find an attempted reconstruction of "Q" in Robert J. Miller (ed), *The Complete Gospels*.

Q is almost entirely a sayings gospel recording things that Jesus allegedly said.

Nowhere in Q is it intimated that Jesus was the Messiah or the Son of God. This is a powerful indicator that Q is a very early document which predates or ignores the Jesus movement's campaign to turn Jesus into the Messiah and the Son of God.

Like the Gospel of Mark, Q starts off with John the Baptist and has no tales of a baby Jesus or a resurrected Jesus.

The Gospel of Matthew

The Gospel of Matthew is a blend of the Gospel of Mark, "Q" (see above), and some material that is distinctive to Matthew which academics have labeled "M".

This Gospel repeats about 90% of what is in Mark.

This Gospel is very concerned to portray Jesus as Jewish and often jumps in with quotes from the Old Testament to prove how Jesus is the fulfillment of Israelite scriptures. This indicates that this Gospel was originally written with a Jewish readership in mind.

The Gospel of Matthew aims to portray Jesus as a second Moses who has come with a new covenant and to rescue the Jews by sacrificing himself. A few of the parallels Matthew creates:

1. The Pharaoh slaughtered all the Israelite boys, with only Moses being saved (Exodus Chapters 1-2). Likewise, Matthew has Herod kill all the male babies in Bethlehem with only Jesus being saved (Matt 2:13-18).

2. The great journey of Moses is to come out of Egypt, leading the Israelites. Likewise, Matthew has the baby Jesus spirited away to Egypt so that he too can later come out of Egypt. (Matt 2:13-21).

3. Moses brings down the Ten Commandments from a mountain. Likewise, Jesus proclaims the Beatitudes on a mountain (Matt 5:1).

4. The first five books of the Hebrew Bible (Genesis, Exodus, Leviticus, Numbers, Deuteronomy) are attributed to the authorship of Moses. Likewise, Matthew has Jesus give five major discourses (Matt 5-7, 10, 13, 18, 22-25). This causes the author to mash together things that were almost certainly said at different times.

The writer is also determined to prove that Jesus is the foretold Jewish Messiah. In order to make this case, he doesn't hesitate to radically embellish passages from the Gospel of Mark. Mark 8:29 reads:

> And he asked them, "But who do you say that I
> am?" Peter answered him, "You are the Messiah."

In the Gospel of Mark, Jesus does not reply to Peter's claim. But the writer of the Gospel of Matthew transubstantiates this simple Markan passage into divine proof that Jesus is the Messiah and the Son of God and that, moreover, Peter would become the legitimate head of the burgeoning first-century Jesus movement:

> He said to them, "But who do you say that I am?"
> Simon Peter replied, "You are the Messiah, the
> Son of the living God." And Jesus answered him,
> "Blessed are you, Simon Bar-Jonah! For flesh and
> blood has not revealed this to you, but my Father
> who is in heaven. And I tell you, you are Peter, and
> on this rock I will build my church, and the gates
> of hell shall not prevail against it. I will give you
> the keys of the kingdom of heaven, and whatever
> you bind on earth shall be bound in heaven, and
> whatever you loose on earth shall be loosed in
> heaven." (Matt 16:15-19)

In a gymnastic feat of double-think, in order to make his case that Jesus had the genetic credentials to be the second Moses and the Messiah, Matthew commences his Gospel with a family tree starting off with Abraham, proceeding through King David and ending up with Joseph then Jesus (Matt 1:1-16)... and then he immediately proceeds to say that Jesus was not the son of Joseph but was a son of the Holy Spirit (Matt:1:18-21).

The Gospel of Luke

Luke (1:1-4) starts off his Gospel specifically admitting that he is creating a composite Gospel based on previous writings:

> Many have undertaken to draw up an account of the things that have been fulfilled among us, just as they were handed down to us by those who from the first were eyewitnesses and servants of the word. With this in mind, since I myself have carefully investigated everything from the beginning, I too decided to write an orderly account for you, most excellent Theophilus, so that you may know the certainty of the things you have been taught.

Luke's Gospel is a blend of the Gospel of Mark, Q, and material distinctive to this Gospel referred to by scholars as "L".

Luke reproduces about 50% of the Gospel of Mark.

Luke's story has a more universal feel. He seems to be writing with both a Jewish and Gentile readership in mind. Accordingly, he deletes the Markan episode most likely to cause offense to Gentiles: the story of the Gentile woman who comes to Jesus to beg for help for her possessed daughter (Mark 7:24-30).

Like Matthew, Luke has a nativity story at the beginning (though a completely different one) and resurrection material at the back end.

Like Matthew, Luke had access to a far more pristine version of the Gospel of Mark than we do. As such, it is possible that some of the Markan material found in Luke is actually truer to the original version of Mark than extant versions of the Gospel of Mark. For instance, the earliest known versions of the Gospel of Luke record Jesus's baptism by the Holy Spirit in this way:

> "And it so happened, when all the people were baptized, and after Jesus had been baptized and while he was praying, that the sky opened up, and

the holy spirit came down on him in bodily form
like a dove, and a voice came from the sky, "You
are my son, today I have become your father."

- Luke 3:21-22. Translation from Robert
J. Miller (ed), *The Complete Gospels*.

There is no reason why Luke would have altered a passage in Mark in this direction so, just possibly, it is more like the original Markan passage than the version of Mark that we now have:

And a voice came from heaven, "You are my
beloved Son; with you I am well pleased."

- Mark 1:9-11

Later versions of Luke were altered by scribes to make that passage more doctrinally correct, so now Bibles generally record the words in Luke as: "You are my beloved Son; with you I am well pleased."

The other big difference in this account of the baptism is that, in Luke, there is a noticeable time gap: first there is Jesus's baptism in water, and only later does the Holy Spirit descend while Jesus is praying. (See Appendix One.)

The Gospel of John

The Gospel of John is out-there different to the first three Gospels. The Gospel of John is based on a very different tradition. It hints that it owes its authority to "the disciple whom Jesus loved the most" (John??).

The whole thrust of the Gospel of John is to prove that Jesus was the Son of God and it frankly admits to this bias:

Now Jesus did many other signs in the presence
of the disciples, which are not written in this
book; but these are written so that you may
believe that Jesus is the Christ, the Son of God,

> and that by believing you may have life in his
> name.
>
> - John 20:30-31

There is a very strong anti-Jewish sentiment in this Gospel. The Jews are the ones totally to blame for the crucifixion of Jesus. Their fault lay in their not recognizing that Jesus was the Son of God and so they committed deicide – killing their own God. This indicates that this Gospel was written with an exclusively Gentile audience in mind.

To give you an idea of how out-there different the Gospel of John is, we only need to consider the phrase "the kingdom of God" – which is what the Jesus of the Synoptic Gospels said his ministry was all about. The phrases "the kingdom of God" or "kingdom of heaven" are mentioned 14 times in Mark, 36 times in Matthew, and 32 times in Luke – noting that Matthew and Luke are both far longer than Mark. That same phrase – "the kingdom of God" – appears a grand total of two times in the entire Gospel of John.

It is very hard to reconcile the earthy preacher in the Gospel of Mark who uses parables with the wordy lecturer in the Gospel of John who uses no parables. The Johannine Jesus seems to talk about himself for an inordinate amount of time. Things that Jesus **may** have said privately to his disciples are wrapped into extremely long discourses. Obviously, these cannot be verbatim accounts.

My opinion is that the Gospel of John probably contains some things that Jesus said privately to his disciples but these have been coalesced, expanded upon, and supplemented in order to form diatribes.

In trying to understand what the historical Jesus was actually like, you have to make a choice between the Jesus in the Gospel of Mark and the Jesus in the Gospel of John. The general academic consensus is that the Gospel of John is extraordinarily problematic as a guide to the life and character of the historical Jesus. In line with this, I only cite a few passages from the Gospel of John.

The Christian Church through the ages has largely gone with the Jesus of the Gospel of John.

The Letters of the Apostle Paul (50 to 58 AD)

If you read the epistles of Paul after reading the Gospels, you tend to think, "Why didn't he cite the words of Jesus more?"

It needs to be realized that Paul never read any of the Gospels because he was writing before they were widely available.

Scholarly experts now consider that only seven epistles in the New Testament can reliably be attributed to Paul. In probable chronological order, they are:

1. First letter to the Thessalonians
2. Letter to the Galatians
3. Letter to the Philippians
4. Letter to Philemon
5. First Letter to the Corinthians
6. Second Letter to the Corinthians
7. Letter to the Romans

If you want to get a handle on understanding Paul, read these seven letters in the above order.

Of the other epistles traditionally ascribed to Paul:

- Colossians and Ephesians are considered to be written by students of Paul with a good grasp of his ideas.
- The second letter to the Thessalonians is considered to be an inept rewriting of an original Pauline letter.

- The letter to Titus and both letters to Timothy are considered to be clearly not by Paul.

See Garry Wills, *What Paul Meant* pp.15-16.

Non-biblical Sources: The Nag Hammadi Library

In December 1945, an astounding discovery was made near Nag Hammadi in Egypt. Locals digging for fertilizer accidentally uncovered a sealed earthenware jar containing thirteen leather-bound papyrus books and some pages torn from another book. These books had been sealed up for centuries. It is theorized that they were hidden there in the fourth century because of an official church clampdown on "heretical" Christian texts.

The texts were written in Coptic, this being the language of Egypt at that time. It is likely that they were all translations from Greek.

Some of these books are "early Christian Gnostic" texts with elaborate stories about creation and angels, etc, etc. They are painful to read and not much use for shedding light on the life of Jesus or anything else. Not to put too fine a point on it: they are junk. But there are a few extremely noteworthy exceptions.

The Gospel of Thomas (date in dispute)

There were existing fragments of the Gospel of Thomas in Greek but finding a full version in Coptic at Nag Hammadi was the pearl beyond price.

It seems to have been the most revered of the Nag Hammadi texts as it was written on the best-quality papyrus.

It is a "sayings Gospel" – being a collection of 114 sayings attributed to Jesus.

I have used the Thomas O. Lambdin translation from James M. Robinson (ed), *The Nag Hammadi Library*.

The dating of this Gospel is tricky because it is a collection of sayings and, as such, is more vulnerable to having more sayings added to it with the passing of years. I would argue for a very early date, not many years after the death of Jesus.

(For more on dating this Gospel, see the Wikipedia article on the Gospel of Thomas.)

The Gospel of Philip (any time from 150 to 350 AD)

Not much of a "Gospel" in the sense that it has nothing on Jesus's life and very few sayings that are even attributed to him but it is pure gold as the reflections and observations of a Christian mystic or, more likely, a number of Christian mystics.

The title "Gospel of Philip" is actually a modern attribution. The text doesn't have a title and happens to mention the disciple Philip.

Both the Patterson Brown and the Wesley W. Isenberg (WI) translations can be found at

http://gospelofthomas.nazirene.org/philip.htm. I mainly use the Patterson Brown translation. When I use the Isenberg translation, I specify this by "WI" but I still reference the numbering of the Paterson Brown translation.

The Gospel of Mary (second century or late first century – some scholars date it even earlier than this)

The contents of this gospel tie in with the idea that Jesus gave secret teachings to his disciples. This gospel intimates that the disciple whom Jesus loved the most was Mary.

Significant slabs of it are missing but it definitely gives the impression that the proper Christian path is one of inner spiritual growth.

I have used the translation in James M. Robinson (ed), *The Nag Hammadi Library* pp. 293-296.

Non-biblical Sources: Other

Josephus, Antiquities of the Jews (93-94 AD)

Josephus was an Israelite army officer in the Jewish-Roman War of 66-73 AD. He managed to make a timely extraction of himself from the routed Jewish forces, dodged a suicide pact, and transferred his allegiance to Rome. He ended up living in Rome where, in the last quarter of the 1st Century, he wrote a number of works about the Jews. These have become crucial to the understanding of Jewish life in that era. His writings include *Antiquities of the Jews* in which he mentions both John the Baptist and Jesus.

One of his two mentions of Jesus is generally accepted as genuine. It is about the stoning of James, "the brother of Jesus, who was called Christ" (Antiquities 20:9.1). The other mention is generally considered to have been significantly doctored by some later Christian true believer. See the Wikipedia article, "Josephus on Jesus".

Josephus's passage on John the Baptist is considered genuine:

> Now some of the Jews thought that the destruction of Herod's army came from God, and that very justly, as a punishment of what he did against John, that was called the Baptist: for Herod slew him, who was a good man, and commanded the Jews to exercise virtue, both as to righteousness towards one another, and piety towards God, and so to come to baptism; for that the washing [with water] would be acceptable to

him, if they made use of it, not in order to the putting away [or the remission] of some sins [only], but for the purification of the body; supposing still that the soul was thoroughly purified beforehand by righteousness. Now when [many] others came in crowds about him, for they were very greatly moved [or pleased] by hearing his words, Herod, who feared lest the great influence John had over the people might put it into his power and inclination to raise a rebellion, (for they seemed ready to do any thing he should advise,) thought it best, by putting him to death, to prevent any mischief he might cause, and not bring himself into difficulties, by sparing a man who might make him repent of it when it would be too late. Accordingly he was sent a prisoner, out of Herod's suspicious temper, to Macherus, the castle I before mentioned, and was there put to death. Now the Jews had an opinion that the destruction of this army was sent as a punishment upon Herod, and a mark of God's displeasure to him. (Flavius Josephus, *Jewish Antiquities* 18. 5. 2. Translation by William Whiston).

The Gospel of the Hebrews (early 2nd Century)

Regrettably, only small fragments of the Gospel of the Hebrews survive in critiques of it by early Church Fathers such as Jerome and Origen. See Robert J. Miller (ed), *The Complete Gospels*, pp. 425-434.

The Upanishads and other mystic writings

I have also drawn on the writings of mystics from Christian and other traditions. See the Select Bibliography.

214

My Source

In the beginning and in the end, there is one seminal reason I ended up writing this book: the inner work I have done and the experiences that came from that. In 1991, I had a series of unanticipated experiences which set me on a path – a very winding path – which led to the writing of this book. Without those experiences, no book.

If you are interested to know more about my inner journey, go to www.renlexander.com.

Appendix Three

Sexing spirituality

Let me make this plain:

- God is not a male. Nor is "He" a female.
- The Holy Spirit is not male. Nor is it female.
- Souls are not female.

They are what they are.

However, we on this earthly plane are trying to grasp at an understanding of these spiritual entities in earthly terms.

Mystics – both male and female – have tended to refer to the soul as feminine. Concepts that come up are "the bride" and, in reference to the purified soul, "virgin". Compared to the might of God, the soul is comparatively weaker, more vulnerable, more receptive, more empathetic. In common earthly ways of thinking, it is more towards the feminine end of the spectrum.

Accordingly, by contrast, God and the Holy Spirit tend to be cast into the masculine role and often receive masculine pronouns. In describing the act of Union of the soul with Spirit, the Holy Spirit is sometimes referred to as "the bridegroom". (See Part IV: Realizing the kingdom of God, "Baptism by the Holy Spirit".)

Interestingly, if we were to compare God and the Holy Spirit, we would tend to refer to the Holy Spirit as feminine in comparison to God. Indeed, the Gospel of Philip in places refers to the Holy Spirit in the feminine, as does the Gospel of the Hebrews. (See Appendix Two.)

The term "the kingdom of God" is the traditional translation of the Greek phrase "*Basileia tou theou*". "*Basileia*" does not actually have a sexist connotation in the original Greek – it could equally refer to "queendom". I have persisted with the traditional translation of "kingdom of God" as I felt that changing that translation would add yet another layer of difficulty to arriving at a correct understanding of the mystic teachings of Jesus. Arguably "domain of God" or "realm of God" would be far better translations.

Acknowledgments

I am humbled by my debt of gratitude to so many people living and dead... every mystic whom I have quoted in this book... Carl Jung... the author of the Gospel of Mark... the author (or authors) of the Gospel of Philip... the author of the Gospel of Matthew for preserving the Beatitudes.

Ahrara Bhakti, without you, quite possibly no book.

Karen Daniels... thank you.

Pamela Matthews, my rock and fellow soul-traveler, with whom I swapped inner work sessions for 14 years.

Laurence Harrould who very kindly read an early version of the manuscript and patiently attempted to convey the essence and history of the spiritual path of his race and religion. His thoughtful input has, I hope, resulted in a more empathetic rendering of the Israelite religion up to the time of Jesus.

The teachers of the classes I did at the then Universal Christian Gnostic Movement. They helped me make greater sense of my inner journey. Unfortunately, they also told me that I couldn't have had that journey because it wasn't done using their techniques so I had to leave their classes... but I didn't leave my gratitude behind.

And so many of the authors of the books in the Bibliography. In particular, I would like to make a respectful nod to Bart D. Ehrman who has produced so many works based around the received academic view on Jesus: that Jesus was preaching the coming of an imminent apocalypse (the coming of "the kingdom of God"). I have benefited greatly from the clarity of his writings and lectures.

Select Bibliography

Almaas, A.H., *Essence. The Diamond Approach to Inner Realization*, (Red Wheel Weiser: 1986).

Armstrong, Karen, *A History of God. The 4000-Year Quest of Judaism, Christianity and Islam* (Ballantine Books: New York, 1993).

Fields of Blood: Religion and the History of Violence (Alfred A. Knopf: 2014)

Aslan, Reza, *Zealot. The Life and Times of Jesus of Nazareth* (Random House: New York, 2013).

Besant, Annie, *Esoteric Christianity* (Theosophical Society: 1905; 2nd edition)

Easwaran, E., (transl), *The Upanishads* (Nilgiri Press: Tomales, California, 1987).

Eckhart, Meister, *Eckhart: A Modern Translation*, translated by Raymond B. Blakney (HarperTorch: 1986).

Selected Writings, translated by Oliver Davies (Penguin, 1994).

The Complete Mystical Works of Meister Eckhart, translated and edited by Maurice O'C Walshe (The Crossroads Publishing Company: New York, 2009).

Ehrman, Bart D., *The Orthodox Corruption of Scripture. The Effect of Early Christological Controversies on the Text of the New Testament* (Oxford University Press: New York, 1993).

Jesus. Apocalyptic Prophet of the New Millennium (Oxford University Press: 1999).

Lost Christianities: The Battles for Scripture and the Faiths We Never Knew (Oxford University Press: 2003).

Misquoting Jesus: The story behind who changed the Bible and why (HarperSanFrancisco: 2005).

The Lost Gospel of Judas Iscariot (Oxford University Press: 2006).

Peter, Paul and Mary Magdalene: The Followers of Jesus in History and Legend (Oxford University Press: 2008).

Jesus, Interrupted. Revealing the Hidden Contradictions in the Bible (and Why We Don't Know About Them) (HarperCollins eBooks: 2009).

Forged: Writing in the Name of God – Why the Bible's Authors Are Not Who We Think They Are (HarperCollins: 2011).

Did Jesus Exist? The Historical Argument for Jesus of Nazareth (HarperOne: 2012)

How Jesus Became God: The Exaltation of a Jewish Preacher from Galilee (HarperOne: 2014).

James, William, *The Varieties of Religious Experience: A Study in Human Nature* (Longmans, Green & Co: 1902).

Jung, C.G., *Aion. Researches into the Phenomenology of the Self,* translated by R.F.C. Hull (2nd edition; Princeton University Press: Princeton, 1968).

Answer to Job, translated by R.F.C. Hull (2nd edition; Princeton University Press: Princeton, 1969).

Levine, Amy-Jill, Dale C. Allison Jr and John Dominic Crossan (ed.), *The Historical Jesus in Context* (Princeton University Press: Princeton, 2006).

Miller, R.J. (ed), *The Complete Gospels. Annotated Scholars Version* (Revised and expanded edition; HarperSanFrancisco: San Francisco, 1994).

O'Reilly, Bill, and Martin Dugard, *Killing Jesus. A History* (Macmillan 2013).

Plotinus   *The Enneads* as translated in W.R. Inge, *The Philosophy of Plotinus* (3rd Edition; Longmans, Green & Co: New York: 1929).

Robinson, James M. (ed), *The Nag Hammadi Library* (HarperCollins: 1981).

Schweitzer, Albert, *The Quest of the Historical Jesus* (1906). You can download it for free from www.gutenberg.org. There is also a free, very good talking book version at www.librivox.com.

St John of the Cross, *The Collected Works of Saint John of the Cross*, translated by Kieran Kavanaugh & Otilio Rodriguez (Revised edition; Institute of Carmelite Studies: Washington, 1991).

St Teresa Avila, *The Interior Castle* (Christian Classics Ethereal Library). Available for free at www.ccel.org. The section of the most interest is the last one, "The Seventh Mansions".

Stace, W.T., (ed) *The Teachings of the Mystics* (Mentor Books: New York, 1960).

Steiner, Rudolf, *Christianity as Mystical Fact* (1902).

   Approaching the Mystery of Golgotha (1914).

   Autobiography: The Story of My Life (1928).

Free talking book versions available at www.rudolfsteineraudio.com.

Wills, Garry, *What Jesus Meant* (Viking Penguin: 2006).

What Paul Meant (Viking Penguin: 2007).

What the Gospels Meant (Viking Penguin: 2008).

Online resources:

www.biblehub.com Excellent website - particularly useful for checking comparative translations.

www.biblestudytools.com Excellent search engine. Very useful for checking such things as word usage frequency.

www.ccel.com Christian Classics Ethereal Library. Many free out-of-copyright resources. Impressive collection.

www.earlychristianwritings.com A very wide range of early Christian literature for free.

www.gutenberg.org Thousands of free out-of-copyright books. For instance, Albert Schweitzer's *The Quest of the Historical Jesus*.

www.librivox.org Out-of-copyright talking books.

www.wikipedia.com A wonderful starting resource for any subject to do with Biblical studies.

You can also purchase university-level courses on Bible studies, Jewish history and Christian history from www.thegreatcourses.com. These are done by top-level academics. Highly recommended...

The Jesus Code is part of

The Meaning of Life series.

Dr Ren Lexander's **The Meaning of Life** series is the most comprehensive and complete look at the question of the meaning of life in history. It covers psychology, spirituality, philosophy and much more.

It presents the final answer to the questions:

- What is the meaning of life?

- And how then can I create an ultimately meaningful life?

    The most important book series you will ever read.

"What is the meaning of life?

This is a question that concerns each and every one of us in the most piercing and dramatic way possible – for in the answer to this question lies the path to a truly meaningful life for each one of us."

This book examines common ideas about the meaning of life – ideas that have shaped individual lives and shaped the history of our planet: ideas such as "life is about preparation for the hereafter", "life is about the pursuit of pleasure" and "life is meaningless".

We shall see that, in the end, there are only two rational answers to the question of "What is the meaning of life?"

And one of these is that life is meaningless.

"Life begins on the other side of despair."

– Jean-Paul Sartre

Without question, one of the most important books you will ever read.

This book explains how a confrontation with meaninglessness (despair, depression, etc.) can lead to a new and better you... and a new and more meaningful life.

If you yourself are going through depression, despair, disillusionment, this is the book you most need to read.

Or... should you know someone who is in a confrontation with meaninglessness, this is the book you most need to receive.

WARNING!

"For many readers, reading this book will be one of the most confronting experiences of their lives. Prior to starting to read it, please have a source of psychological and/or emotional support lined up – whether this be a professional therapist or just someone you can talk to. I do not recommend that you read this book with a partner as the danger is that at least one of you will start trying to talk the other one out of reading it (as a way of talking themselves out of reading it)."

The ultimate answer to the question

What is the meaning of life?

The Journey of the Souls

and

the
Meaning
of
Life

Ren Lexander

Part of The Meaning of Life

Well... it would be a great shame if all this contemplation of the biggest question of all time didn't lead to a few jokes and whimsical observations.

Keep up to date with the latest releases:

renlexander.com

Printed in Great Britain
by Amazon

27610286R00136